THE SACRAMENTS

Thomas Richstatter, O.F.M.

THE SACRAMENTS
How Catholics Pray

ST.
ANTHONY
MESSENGER
PRESS

CINCINNATI, OH

Nihil Obstat: Rev. Donald Miller, O.F.M.
Rev. Edward J. Gratsch

Imprimi Potest: Rev. John Bok, O.F.M.
Provincial

Imprimatur: Most Reverend Carl K. Moeddel, V.G.
Archdiocese of Cincinnati, April 10, 1995

"Liturgy: Why I Go to Church," *Faith Notes*, St. Meinrad, Ind.: Abbey Press, 1991.

Sections of Chapter One have been published previously in "Sacraments: It All Starts With Jesus," *Catholic Update*, Cincinnati: St. Anthony Messenger Press, August 1993.

Sections of Chapter Two have been published previously in "Lent: A 40-Day Retreat: Rediscovering Your Baptismal Call," *Catholic Update*, Cincinnati: St. Anthony Messenger Press, February 1990.

Sections of Chapter Three have been published previously in "A Walk Through the Mass: A Step-by-Step Explanation," *Catholic Update*, Cincinnati: St. Anthony Messenger Press, August 1989.

Sections of Chapter Four have been published previously in "The Sacrament of the Eucharist: What Has Happened to My Devotion?" *Catholic Update*, Cincinnati: St. Anthony Messenger Press, September 1992.

Sections of Chapter Five have been published previously in "A Tour of a Catholic Church," *Catholic Update*, Cincinnati: St. Anthony Messenger Press, March 1991.

Sections of Chapter Six have been published previously in *The Reconciliation of Penitents: A Study of the Structural Elements of the Communal Rite of Penance*, Washington, D.C.: Federation of Diocesan Liturgical Commissions, 1987, and in "The Gift of Reconciliation: Ten Tips for Better Confessions," *Catholic Update*, Cincinnati: St. Anthony Messenger Press, August 1990.

Sections of Chapter Seven have been published previously in "The New Rite for Anointing the Sick," *Catholic Update*, Cincinnati: St. Anthony Messenger Press, May 1984, and in *Would You Like to Be Anointed?* Cincinnati: St. Anthony Messenger Press, 1987.

Sections of Chapter Eight have been published previously in "Holy Orders: What Is the Priest's Role Today?" *Catholic Update*, Cincinnati: St. Anthony Messenger Press, June 1981, and in "Lay Ministry: Not Just for a Chosen Few," *Catholic Update*, Cincinnati: St. Anthony Messenger Press, August 1991.

Sections of Chapter Twelve have been published previously in "Lay Ministry: Not Just for a Chosen Few," *Catholic Update*, Cincinnati: St. Anthony Messenger Press, August 1991.

Cover design by Leslie Brod
Book design by Mary Alfieri

ISBN 0-86716-176-0

Published by St. Anthony Messenger Press
Printed in the U.S.A.

With special thanks to
Bryan Patrick Vaughn
for his support and
helpful suggestions

Contents

Symbol and Ritual

May God give you peace and all things good!
(Greeting of Saint Francis of Assisi)

Some of my friends who are not Catholic tell me that when they attend services in a Catholic church they find our way of praying—well, "complicated," to say the least. Many of them say that their Sunday worship consists of singing a hymn, reading together from the Bible, listening to a sermon and singing a final hymn. Compared to that, I guess our way of praying is complicated. But I grew up with this Catholic way of praying; I don't find it complicated at all. And I think that it can be rather easily explained.

That is what I would like to do in this book. I would like to walk with you on a tour through the sacraments and try to make them less complicated by explaining the meaning of the rites, by giving the reasons why we do what we do, and by telling you something of the history of these ceremonies to help you understand how Catholics pray.

I am writing this book partly for my non-Catholic friends who sometimes attend Catholic services. Perhaps some of you are married to Catholics and attend Catholic services rather regularly; maybe you are merely curious. Some of you may be thinking about becoming Catholic yourselves.

I am also writing for those Catholics who, while they are baptized and readily acknowledge their Catholic identity, need a quick refresher course in the sacraments. This book is *not* for Catholics who want to know why things have changed or why the Mass isn't like it used to be. The perspective here is different. This book is for people who want to know how Catholics pray *now*.

Neither is this book for those Catholics whose experience has taken them far beyond the "first look" presented here. This book is *only* a first look at how Catholics pray; it is not a theology of the sacraments or a catechism. I hope, however, that this "first look" will whet your appetite to know more about the sacraments and to read books that do treat them in a fuller and more complete way.

The Catholic Church has recently published an official summary of Catholic teaching, the *Catechism of the Catholic Church*. Intended primarily for bishops and other teachers of the Catholic faith, it could be useful to you also. I have given *Catechism* references at the end of each chapter of this book for those who would like to clarify any issues that may arise from reading or discussions.

A Few Key Terms

Traveling in a foreign land is often made much easier if you know the local language, or at least a few key words and phrases. Similarly, our tour through the sacraments will be easier if I explain a few key terms.

The word *sacrament* will be the topic of the first chapter, and the words *Mass* and *Eucharist* will be discussed shortly after that. Here I would like to introduce three terms: *The Second Vatican Council*, *ritual* and *liturgy*.

The Second Vatican Council
Anyone who sets out to learn more about how Catholics pray will quickly come upon the Second Vatican Council. In 1959 Pope John XXIII announced his intention to call together all the bishops in communion with him throughout the world. The purpose of this meeting was: (1) to discuss ways in which new vigor could be given to Christian life; (2) to adapt Church institutions to the needs of our times; (3) to foster whatever promotes unity among Christians; and (4) to strengthen whatever would help the whole of humanity hear the Good News of Christ. Such a meeting of all the bishops is called a *council*. This particular Council (the twenty-first such meeting

in the Church's history) took place in Vatican City in Rome, and is therefore called the Vatican Council. A similar meeting had been held at the Vatican in 1869-1870; consequently this 1962-1965 meeting is called the *Second* Vatican Council.

The Council issued sixteen major documents. The first of these was the *Constitution on the Liturgy*. This document stated the general principles for a reform of Roman Catholic prayer that radically altered the Catholic worship throughout the world.

The Second Vatican Council is a watershed event for us Catholics. It not only changed the shape and language of our ritual prayers but also changed the way in which we speak about the sacraments. Before the Council, I celebrated Mass in Latin; now I celebrate in the language of the country where I am. Before the Council, I said Mass with my back to the people; now I celebrate facing the people. Before the Council, if I had written a book about the sacraments, it would have been a very different book from this book! The fact that we experience sacraments in a new way has led us to talk about the sacraments in a new way.

For many people 1965 (the close of the Council) was a long time ago. But many Catholics still refer to the prayer forms renewed by the Council as the *new* liturgy. It may seem strange that something which has been in use so long is still being called *new*! But one of the first and most important things to know about the way Catholics pray is that our prayer forms change very slowly. It is good to be aware of this at the very beginning of our tour through the sacraments: It takes a long time to establish new rituals. It takes a long time for Catholics to change their traditional ways of praying.

Ritual Actions

My friend Brad is thinking about becoming a Catholic. A member of a small evangelical Church, he became interested in the Catholic Church through some Catholic friends and started attending Sunday Mass. One day Brad stopped by my house to ask me some questions about the way Catholics act in church. I was struck by Brad's first observation: "Father, the thing that is most different between my Church and your Church is that you

Catholics always seem to know what is going to happen next! In my Church we sit and listen and sing now and then, but in the Catholic Church you have to *know* what to do."

Brad has a good point: We Catholics do know what is going to happen next. One of the basic, distinctive marks of our way of praying is *ritual*: we do things over and over in set ways, and after a while, we know what is going to happen next. When the priest says, "The Lord be with you," the congregation responds without any thought or hesitation, "And also with you." The priest says, "Let us pray," and the congregation stands up.

Our daily lives have rituals also. There are set ways of shaking hands, eating with a fork, responding to a letter. And when we are accustomed to a certain way of doing things we seldom ask *why* we do it that way. For example, on your birthday you probably blow out the candles on your cake. Why? Does it have something to do with that first gasp of breath when you were born and the countless, continuous breaths you have taken from that moment to this birthday? Whatever the meaning of the candles on the birthday cake, I know that I never worry about such things when I blow out the candles on my cake—a thing which is getting increasingly harder to do! It is just part of the celebration, part of what we do to celebrate birthdays. It's a ritual.

We seldom ask *why* when performing rituals. But if a visitor from another culture who had never seen candles on a birthday cake were present at your birthday party, the visitor might well find this custom rather strange and ask, "Why are you doing that?" We Catholics have many ritual actions which we perform at Mass without asking *why*. But when visitors from other Churches come to Mass they will ask lots of *why* questions! I hope this book will help you understand the meaning of some of these ritual actions.

Liturgy: Public Prayer

There are times when we Catholics pray privately as individuals and there are times when we join together and pray together as Church in the name of Christ. This prayer of the Church has come to be called *liturgy*. The word embraces our celebration of Mass and the sacraments, the Liturgy of the

Hours and the liturgical year, music and art.

Liturgy is our *official* prayer, the prayer which expresses who we are as Catholics and how we understand the meaning of Jesus' passion, death and resurrection. In the formal language of the Second Vatican Council, the liturgy is "the means whereby the faithful may express in their lives and manifest to others the mystery of Christ and the real nature of the true Church" (*Constitution on the Sacred Liturgy*, #2). In other words, liturgy makes visible, both to ourselves and to others, who we are and what God wants us to be.

Almost everyone has had some experience of prayer. Most Americans, even those who do not consider themselves "religious," readily acknowledge that they pray—and many pray frequently. In this book, however, we will explore that ritual, repetitious, formal, official, collective, public prayer we call liturgy.

The sacraments are the principal liturgical rites you will encounter if you attend a Catholic Church. The sacraments are such a "special" kind of prayer that many Catholics do not think of them as prayer at all! Some Catholics would be surprised at the title of this book, *Sacraments: How Catholics Pray*. They think of sacraments as something we "receive," not a way in which we pray.

A lot of people tell me that they go to church to pray—meaning to pray privately. Nothing wrong with that. But I can pray at home. In fact, I pray better at home. I pray especially well on long walks down by the river. It takes me a while to get into it, but after a mile or so, God and I have some really good talks—often better than the ones we have in church. I go to church for public prayer—for the liturgy.

Many of my Baptist friends tell me that they go to church to read the Bible and to sing and especially to hear the sermon. I certainly appreciate hearing the Bible proclaimed; I love to sing; and God knows I enjoy a good sermon or homily. But the liturgy is more than all that. Just hearing the Word of God and understanding it isn't enough for me. I am more than my understanding, more than just my head: I want to worship God with my *whole body*. And I think it is my Catholic tradition which makes me want to experience Church in this way.

5

Catholics are big on Incarnation—not just Christmas, though we're big on that, too—but *the* Incarnation: God taking our flesh, coming here to our earth so that we can find God in our very "earthy-ness": "And the Word became flesh and lived among us, and we have his glory, the glory as of the Father's only son, full of grace and truth" (John 1:14).

Catholics believe in a God who knows all about us: knows what it is to be happy, to be sad, to worry, to cry, to be disappointed, to be like us in every way. "Because [Jesus] himself was tested by what he suffered, he is able to help those who are being tested" (Hebrews 2:18).

Jesus knew what we are all about—and not just knew in his head, but also in his body: knew the strain of lifting a heavy table, the sweat of working in the desert sun, the pain of hunger, the embrace of friends, the joyful taste of rich red wine! God dwelt among us, and in that Incarnation, that taking flesh, God wants to save not just our "souls" but also our bodies, our nations, our ancestors, our whole earth. Mountains and hills, fire and heat, dew and rain, birds and beasts, wild and tame, "bless the Lord!" (see Daniel 3:57-88).

For Catholics the Incarnation means that the very stuff of this earth has been taken up into the Kingdom of God. The things of this earth are not distractions from praying or hindrances to our worship but are the very way—media, means, symbols, instruments, sacraments—for liturgical prayer.

Catholics worship not just with their heads but with the things of the earth: bread and wine, water and oil, coming together and going apart, standing still and processing forward, lighting candles and smelling flowers, even dust and ashes! That's *liturgical* prayer—prayer with the body, the earth, ritual, song, celebration.

In the liturgy we not only hear of God's dreams for us, we further act them out; we are taken up into those dreams. I hear of God's dreams of justice for all peoples of all nations; in Holy Communion I see how the Body and Blood of the Lord is broken and shared and how everyone receives "enough"—the rich and the poor, the young and the old, the hungry and the weak. And the contrast between the Table of the Lord and the table of this world (where very few have "enough," indeed millions are starving!) forces me to rethink my ideas of justice and charity.

We don't just pray, "Thy kingdom come": We experience what the Kingdom promises. We don't just talk about Holy Thursday: We eat and drink. We don't just talk about Good Friday: We are sacrifice. We don't just talk about Easter: We are risen in the promise of Christ. That is what liturgy is: living out our story.

The statement of the Bishops' Committee on the Liturgy, *Environment and Art in Catholic Worship* (#16), reminds us that a culture such as ours, "oriented to efficiency and production has made us insensitive to the symbolic function of persons and things." This is one of the reasons why many Americans find liturgical prayer difficult: It demands a sensitivity to the *symbolic function* of persons and things. Symbol is the very language of liturgy. For people who are schooled in the scientific, the practical and countable, symbols and rituals are often "foreign" and take some getting used to.

Symbols can carry more meaning than a declarative statement or scientific formula or theological dogma. When I received Holy Communion for the first time at the age of six, I did so with great reverence. I "knew what I was doing." Today I certainly know more about the Eucharist then I did then. I have written books on the Eucharist. But the same liturgical action, sharing a piece of bread with the other worshipers at Sunday Mass, is able to hold all these meanings—and more besides! That is the beauty of liturgy: Liturgy means more than we can ever understand it to mean. A symbol "says" more than mere words could ever say.

Often at weddings, when I watch the couple exchange rings, I wonder at what that means. The meaning is more than the ring itself. I have seen seventy-dollar rings and I have seen seven thousand-dollar rings. The meaning is not in the gold or the price. I am glad that the Catholic ceremony doesn't try to explain anything at this point of the ceremony. Even the best of words are inadequate.

The Bishops' statement *Environment and Art in Catholic Worship* (#16) adds that the American "cultural emphasis on individuality and competition has made it more difficult for us

7

to appreciate the liturgy as a *personal-communal* experience. As a consequence, we tend to identify anything private and individual as 'personal.' But, by inference, anything communal and social is considered impersonal." This is another American difficulty with liturgy: Because liturgy is public and communal, some see it as impersonal and distant. Good liturgy is never private, but good liturgy is always personal. I have experienced private prayer and public prayer; both can be my personal prayer. I can't imagine what impersonal prayer would be; but insofar as I can imagine it, I am sure I wouldn't want it.

I'd hate to go to church some Sunday and find I was the only one who came! I need the witness of other folks. There are times when I am not too sure that I want to get out of bed and go to church, but I can look around the church and see that others, by their very presence there, tell me, "This is important to us, too." The presence of others is especially helpful when I know how their faith is important in their lives: How Jane has found strength from her faith following her miscarriage; how Henry faithfully comes to Mass every Sunday even after his divorce, and how our faith community is one of his major supports in dealing with the loneliness. My faith is strengthened by the faith of the other worshipers—especially when I know them and know of their faith. Liturgy is something bigger than just *my* prayer and *my* faith.

The liturgy constantly reminds me that I am taken up into something much bigger than myself. At Mass we pray, "Lord, remember your Church throughout the world..." and we recall the name of our bishop. The liturgy is something we do with the bishop, whom I don't think of very often and see even less often. But this Mass is his liturgy and the worship of this whole diocese. We also ask God to remember the bishop of Rome, whom I see even less frequently. This is his worship also, and the liturgy of the diocese of Rome and the worship of millions of Catholics all over the earth: Catholics in Zaire and Australia, Catholics in Israel and Iran, Catholics in New York City and Catholics in Tell City, Indiana—in every place and in every age!

What we are doing now is what we will be doing forever when,

freed from every shadow of death,
we shall take our place in the new creation....
(Eucharistic Prayer for Masses of Reconciliation I)

There we will be seated at table with:

people of every race, language, and way of life
to share in the one eternal banquet
with Jesus Christ the Lord.
(Eucharistic Prayer for Masses of Reconciliation II)

How to Use This Book

Each chapter is relatively short and covers one topic. I have
tried to select the information which would be most useful for a
"first look." Frequently I will use words from the prayers of the
liturgy as a source for our understanding of the sacraments.
This practice has a long tradition among Catholics, as
evidenced in the *Catechism of the Catholic Church*. As the
topic of the book is prayer, it might be good actually to pray
with each chapter. At the end of each I have given a few
suggestions "For Prayer" to stimulate your own prayer.

Discussion can help to clarify ideas even if the "discussion"
is only an imaginary conversation with yourself. Some readers
will be exploring the sacraments in a discussion group or
perhaps during their catechumenate. With each chapter I have
given some questions to start the conversation under the
heading "For Reflection and Discussion."

Finally, at the end of each chapter I make a few suggestions
"For Further Information." For the most part, I have listed
books that I myself have found useful. I have also listed the
numbers in the *Catechism of the Catholic Church* where more
information on the topic may be found.

May God be with us as we begin this journey through the
sacraments, the way Catholics pray!

FOR PRAYER

Jesus, be with me
  as I begin this journey through the sacraments.
I need to understand how Catholics pray.
Most of all, Jesus, help me to pray.
Help me to pray more earnestly, more sincerely.
Help me discover new ways to pray
  that will make my love for you grow
    and help me realize even more your immense love for me.

FOR REFLECTION AND DISCUSSION

1) Where do you do your best praying?

2) Do you prefer praying alone or praying with others?

3) Recall your best experience of communal prayer. What caused it to be such a good experience?

FOR FURTHER READING

Tad Guzie, *The Book of Sacramental Basics*. Ramsey, N.J.: Paulist Press, 1981.

Gilbert Ostdiek, *Catechesis for Liturgy*. Washington, D.C.: Pastoral Press, 1986.

Catechism of the Catholic Church, "The Celebration of the Christian Mystery" (#1066-1075); "Celebrating the Church's Liturgy" (#1136-1199).

CHAPTER ONE

It All Starts With Jesus:
The Sacrament and the Sacraments

As we take our first steps on our journey through the
sacraments, it might be good to say what the word *sacrament*
means. Catholics my age all memorized the definition from the
Baltimore Catechism: "A sacrament is an outward sign
instituted by Christ to give grace." While this is a good
definition, I think it might be more helpful to enter through a
different door.

The first thing I want to say about the way Catholics pray is
that Catholics *do* believe in Jesus and Catholics *do* read the
Bible. We are sometimes accused of being caught up in empty
rituals and neglecting Jesus and the Bible, yet nothing could be
further from the truth. Our Catholic faith and way of
praying—indeed all Christian faith—begins with Jesus and is
based on the Bible. It all starts with Jesus. So our journey
through the sacraments will start at the beginning, with Jesus.

In the Beginning...

The loving God who created us wants to be present to us, to be
with us. Lovers want to be together. God knows how hard it is
for us to love someone we cannot see or touch. And so, in
God's mysterious plan, the invisible God took flesh, came
among us and became truly human. Central to the mystery of
Christmas (and Catholic prayer centers on Christmas and
Easter) is the realization that God comes to us and we come to
God in the flesh: through our bodies in the created world.

The invisible God, whom no eye has seen, was seen in the humanity of Jesus. God, whose wonder and love are beyond our imagination, wished to become visible and close to us. This is the very basic, root meaning of *sacrament*: making the invisible visible.

Saint Augustine (d. 430) calls sacraments "visible signs of invisible grace." Our understanding of sacrament starts with "making the invisible visible." As we pray at Christmas Mass,

> In the wonder of the incarnation
> your eternal Word has brought to the eyes of faith
> a new and radiant vision of your glory.
> In him we see our God made visible
> and so are caught up in love of the God we cannot see.
> (Preface I)

The first step in understanding the meaning of *sacrament* is to see Jesus himself, in his humanity, as the first and original sacrament. It all starts with Jesus: Jesus himself is sacrament, the visible sign of the invisible God.

From Jesus to Church

Sometimes I hear people say: "Wouldn't it have been wonderful to have lived at the very time of Jesus, to have seen him in the flesh and moved among the disciples!" We Catholics believe that, in the wonderful plan of God, we who live in the twentieth century are not at a disadvantage from those people who were alive when Jesus walked the earth. We, today, see Christ and move among the disciples.

This is neither a modern nor a specifically Catholic notion. Saint Paul was born again in the light of the revelation that Christ is still present among us: "I fell to the ground and heard a voice saying to me, 'Saul, Saul, why are you persecuting me?' I replied, 'Who are you, Lord?' Then he said to me, 'I am Jesus of Nazareth whom you are persecuting'" (Acts 22:7-8).

From that moment on Paul realized that Christ cannot be separated from his members. The risen Christ is so identified with the Christian that whatever Paul did to a Christian (whether persecution or blessing) Paul did to Christ himself. The Christian is baptized into Christ and can say with Paul: "[A]nd it is no longer I who live, but it is Christ who lives in me" (Galatians 2:20a).

As Jesus is the original sacrament, so we who are baptized into the risen Christ become sacrament. Today it is Christ's Body the Church which is the primary sacrament, the revelation of the loving plan of God.

The Church itself is sacrament. The sacraments are not so much something we *receive* as something that we *are*. We are sacrament, instruments of grace; we are the ordinary way God graces today's world.

Consequently, this book is not merely about something that Catholics do (sacraments in the plural); it is about the Church itself (*the* sacrament). It is about who we are as Catholics. The sacraments are "outstanding means whereby we express in our lives and manifest to others the mystery of Christ and the real nature of our Church" (*Constitution on the Liturgy*, #2).

God's Dreams for the World

What is it that the sacraments make visible? They make visible the story of God's dreams for the world. "God...sent his Son, the Word made flesh, anointed by the Holy Spirit, to preach the Gospel to the poor, to heal the contrite of heart.... For his humanity united with the Person of the Word, was the instrument of our salvation. Therefore, 'in Christ the perfect achievement of our reconciliation came forth and the fullness of divine worship was given to us' " (*Constitution on the Liturgy*, #5).

We read of God's plan for the world on every page of sacred Scripture. On the very first pages of the Bible we see God creating this magnificent world and all that is in it. God created the universe and from the earth God created an earthling and breathed into it God's own image. And all was at peace.

I like to see in the first chapters of Genesis a threefold harmony: (1) Men and women were at peace *with each other*;

they were naked and not ashamed. (2) The human creatures were at peace *with the earth*; Adam named the animals and tilled the earth, and it brought forth its fruit. And (3) they were at peace *with God*; Adam walked in the garden and talked with God. And it was good. On the first page of the Bible we get a glimpse of the harmony God wants at the end of time: all creation reconciled and at peace.

But sin shatters every layer of the dream: harmony with each other (they accuse each other); with the earth, which must be coaxed to yield up its fruits by human labor; and with God, from whom Adam hid himself.

When the time was ripe, Jesus came to bring the dream of God to completion. He spent his life healing sickness and division. By his death and resurrection he reconciled all things in himself and made it possible for God's plan to be realized. Easter is the promise that the dream will be realized. We enter into this magnificent plan of God by Baptism/Confirmation/ Eucharist, by celebrating the sacraments.

Telling the Story

In this world divided by war and greed we must continually retell the story of God's plan for unity and reconciliation. We must keep the dream of God alive. We, the Church, do this first of all in the celebration of the sacraments. The sacraments are the celebration of our Christian story. This is the principal reason why the proclamation of Scripture is an essential part of every sacramental celebration. Sacraments are worded signs. Scripture is the word, the story which makes the sacramental sign meaningful.

Sacraments celebrate the goodness of all creation—one of the great themes of the Catholic prayer tradition. Material things are good. Our human bodies, our very flesh and bones are good. God took flesh and dwelt among us, and in this mystery of taking on human flesh proclaimed that the things of this earth are not obstacles to God but are intended to be windows to the divine. The magnificence of creation enables us to see something of the wonder, the multiplicity, the superabundance of God.

This theme—creation is good—is key to understanding the way Catholics pray. Catholicism is a *sacramental* religion that prays with bathing and eating, singing and embracing. Sacraments celebrate the goodness, the grace-filled essence, of creation: water and fire, oil and salt, ashes and palm branches, bread and wine. Creation draws us into the very life of the Creator:

> Bless the Lord, all you works of the Lord....
> Bless the Lord, sun and moon....
> Bless the Lord, fire and heat....
> Bless the Lord, ice and cold....
> Bless the Lord, seas and rivers....
> Bless the Lord, you whales and all that swim in the
>   waters....
> Bless the Lord, all wild animals and cattle.... (see
>   Azariah 1:35-65 or Daniel 3:57-88)

How Many Sacraments Are There?

If you ask a Catholic how many sacraments there are, you will probably be told that there are seven: Baptism, Confirmation, Eucharist, Reconciliation, Anointing of the Sick, Marriage and Holy Orders. If Jesus is a sacrament and the Church is a sacrament, does that make *nine* sacraments?

The question "How many sacraments are there?" has received different answers at various periods of our history, depending on what the question meant and how the questioner understood the word *sacrament*.

Today we Americans usually (nearly always!) use numbers as *quantities*. They tell us how much or how many. How much is my gas bill? How many days till Christmas? But numbers can also be used as *qualities*. For example, many people feel that thirteen is unlucky. *Thirteen* in this sense indicates a quality (unlucky) rather than a quantity (twelve plus one). It is not something you can figure out mathematically or explain to a nonbeliever. In our industrial America this qualitative use of numbers sounds strange or superstitious. But this use is quite common in other societies and other historical periods. Numbers as qualities have often been used in religion.

Seven, for example, symbolizes totality. This is an important factor in the Church's speaking of seven sacraments. Four is the number for earth and three is the number for heaven (from the four elements: earth, air, fire and water, and the three Persons in God). When we join earth and heaven, the material and the spiritual, the created and the divine, four and three, we have *all that is*. And so, seven means universality, completeness, totality. When we say that there are seven sacraments we are suggesting in this religious sense that the material universe is a sacrament, that all created things are windows to the divine, that we have all the sacraments we will ever need! (Seven is frequently used in this sense: There are seven gifts of the Holy Spirit. In the Book of Revelation John writes to the seven Churches, that is, to the universal Church.)

Sacraments in the Bible

We do not find the word *sacrament* in the Bible. *Sacrament* is a Latin word; our Christian Scriptures, however, were written in Greek. Hence the word for "sacrament" we find in the Bible is the Greek word *mysterion*, "mystery."

Today the English word *mystery* is frequently used to mean something we cannot understand. ("How she could have all that money and still be so unhappy is a mystery to me.") The Greek word *mysterion* is usually translated in English Bibles as "plan," referring to the wonderful, mysterious plan that God had before creation began, to take flesh in Jesus and to draw all of creation into a harmonious unity so spectacular and breathtaking that the very idea is too wonderful for us, something we can never fully understand. This is the fundamental meaning of "sacrament" in the Bible.

Saint Paul says that it is his life's work to announce and bring to completion this "mystery that has been hidden throughout the ages and generations" (Colossians 1:26a). "Although I am the very least of all the saints, this grace was given to me to bring to the Gentiles the news of the boundless riches of Christ, and to make everyone see what is *the plan of the mystery* hidden for ages in God who created all things; so that through the Church the wisdom of God in its rich variety might now be made known..." (Ephesians 3:8-10a, emphasis added).

When the language of the Church changed from Greek to Latin, the Greek word *mysterion* was sometimes translated by the Latin word *sacramentum*; it is in this word that we find the biblical roots of the word *sacrament*.

For the first eleven centuries of Christian history the word *sacrament* was frequently used in this more general sense, referring to the mysterious plan of God. Little by little specific aspects of this mysterious plan (for example, Eucharist, Baptism, Anointing of the Sick) began to be singled out and called sacraments. In the twelfth century, in the works of teachers such as Hugh of St. Victor (d. 1141) and Peter Lombard (d. 1160), we begin to see the list of the seven actions which Catholics now call sacraments. In 1547, responding to specific questions being asked at the time, the Council of Trent stated: "The sacraments of the new law are seven, no more and no less" (Session VII, Canon 1).

The Presence of God

We cannot understand sacraments without looking at our understanding of grace. Grace has been understood in many different ways in Christian history. Probably most Catholics today think of grace as "a gift of God."

The greatest gift that God can give us is the gift of God's very self, God's personal self-communication. Grace is not so much some*thing* that is given but some*one* who is experienced as present. Sacramental celebrations enable us in faith to touch Grace itself, to contact the all-pervading presence of the loving God who sustains all created things in existence. The sacraments allow us to become conscious and aware of God's greatest gift: the creative, sustaining, loving presence of God.

Our Catholic understanding of sacrament is related to our

17

ideas of grace and presence. All of the sacraments, not just the Eucharist, are celebrations of God's real presence. In celebrating the sacraments we, the Church, proclaim anew the marvelous, mysterious plan (*mysterion, sacramentum*) of God to bring all things together in Christ.

> To accomplish so great a work, Christ is always present in his Church, especially in its liturgical celebrations. He is present in the sacrifice of the Mass, not only in the person of his minister, "the same now offering, through the ministry of priests, who formerly offered himself on the cross," but especially under the eucharistic elements. By his power he is present in the sacraments, so that when a man baptizes it is really Christ himself who baptizes. He is present in his word, since it is he himself who speaks when the holy Scriptures are read in the Church. He is present, lastly, when the Church prays and sings, for he promised: "Where two or three are gathered together in my name, there am I in the midst of them" (Matthew 18:20). (*Constitution on the Liturgy*, #7)

Sacraments proclaim the mysterious, hidden plan of God to bring all things together in Christ. Sacraments are the celebration of the presence of Christ in our midst.

Toward a Definition of a Sacrament

Sacrament is such a complex, dynamic reality that no one is really going to be able to define it adequately. Think, for example, of how you would define Thanksgiving dinner at Grandmother's or the high school prom or the final game of the World Series. These dynamic ritual celebrations are more verb than noun. Definitions are impossible; even lengthy, detailed descriptions fail. After all the defining and describing are over, we are left with: "Well, you would have to be there!" Sacraments are like that. To understand them fully, you have to be there! You have to experience them in person.

18

Contemporary Christians, reflecting on their experience, have given us descriptions of sacrament that can help us reflect on our experience: "A sacrament is a festive action in which Christians assemble to celebrate their lived experience and to call to heart their common story. The action is a symbol of God's care for us in Christ. Enacting the symbol brings us closer to one another in the Church and to the Lord who is there for us."[1]

"Sacraments are symbolic actions manifesting the offer of God's saving love for us in Christ and through the Spirit in the Church. In the sacraments, we respond to God's self-giving and draw closer not only to God but also to one another in the Church."[2]

A description which helped me rethink my idea of sacrament is: "As long as you notice, and have to count the steps, you are not yet dancing but only learning how to dance. A good shoe is a shoe you don't notice. Good reading becomes possible when you do not consciously think about eyes, or light, or print, or spelling. The perfect liturgy would be one we were almost unaware of; our attention would have been on God."[3]

I hope this chapter has helped you see that Mass and the sacraments are not merely something that one "receives" or "goes to." They are *how Catholics pray*. Our focus is not on the ritual. Our attention is on God. God's plan is disclosed. God's people are renewed. Christ's presence is celebrated. Salvation is realized. In celebrating the sacraments we, the Church in today's broken world, keep the dreams of God alive!

FOR PRAYER

O loving God, help me to know your plan for me.
Help me to know my place in your plan for the world.
Help me to dream your dreams.
Help me to keep your dreams alive.
Help me to live a life of generosity,
    of compassion,
    of understanding.

Jesus, you came to us to save us,
    to heal us,
    to love us.
By your cross and resurrection
    you restored the wonderful plan for the destiny of the
      world.
I want to follow you,
    to walk in your footsteps,
    to be an instrument of your peace
    and an ambassador of reconciliation.
Forgive me for the times when I cause division
    rather than peace,
    especially for those times when I _____.
Thank you for the beautiful things which reveal your love,
    and especially, thank you for _____.

FOR REFLECTION AND DISCUSSION

1) Have you read the Bible? Have you read the whole New Testament? How frequently do you read the Bible?

2) Do you see the Bible as *your* story or as stories about people who lived a long time ago?

3) Does reading the Bible influence the way that you pray? What is the relationship between the Bible and your personal prayer?

4) How would you describe God's dreams for the world?

FOR FURTHER INFORMATION

Leonardo Boff, *Sacraments of Life, Life of the Sacraments.* Washington, D.C.: Pastoral Press, 1987.

Bernard Cooke, *Sacraments and Sacramentality.* Mystic, Conn.: Twenty-Third Publications, 1983.

Bernard Lee (General Editor), *Alternative Futures for Worship.* Collegeville, Minn.: The Liturgical Press, 1987.

Kenan Osborne, *Sacramental Theology: A General Introduction.* New York: Paulist Press, 1988.

Catechism of the Catholic Church, "And in Jesus Christ, His Only Son, Our Lord" (#430-455); "The Liturgy: Work of the Holy Trinity" (#1077-1112); "The Paschal Mystery in the Church's Sacraments" (#1113-1134).

Notes

[1] Tad Guzie, *The Book of Sacramental Basics.* New York: Paulist Press, 1981, p. 53.

[2] Richard M. Gula, S.S., *To Walk Together Again.* New York: Paulist Press, 1984, p. 77.

[3] C. S. Lewis, *Letters to Malcolm.* London: Harcourt Brace Jovanovich, 1964, p. 4.

CHAPTER TWO

The Sacraments of Initiation:
Baptism, Confirmation, Eucharist

Everything that Jesus said and did reveals God's mysterious plan for us. Jesus' entire life was salvific. But we often sum up the meaning of his life in the pascal victory: his passion, death and resurrection. At the Eucharist the Holy Thursday words, "Do this in memory of me," tell us to do not only what Jesus did at the Last Supper but also to do what Jesus did throughout his entire life: heal, teach, comfort, be an ambassador of reconciliation (see 2 Corinthians 5:16-21). In the sacraments of initiation (Baptism, Confirmation and Eucharist) we are so identified with the risen Christ that we can say with Saint Paul that "it is no longer I who live, but it is Christ who lives in me" (Galatians 2:20a).

Today it is Christ's Body, the Church, which is the principal sacrament, the principal revelation of the loving plan of God. As the Second Vatican Council teaches, Jesus "rising from the dead, sent his life-giving Spirit upon his disciples and through this Spirit has established his Body, the Church, as the universal sacrament of salvation" (*Constitution on the Church*, #48).

The Church is best seen as sacrament in the celebration of the Eucharist. The Eucharist is not just *one* of the seven sacraments; it is *the* sacrament, for it contains all that we are, all that the Church is, all that Jesus says of God. This is why any tour through the sacraments begins with the Eucharist.

The first time an adult comes to the Eucharist is through the sacraments of Christian initiation: Baptism, Confirmation and Eucharist. Eucharist is the ritual culmination of the initiation process: "The holy Eucharist completes Christian initiation" (*Catechism of the Catholic Church*, #1322). In this chapter we will look at the process of Christian initiation and examine the journey one takes toward first Eucharist. Chapter Four will focus specifically on the meaning of the Eucharist itself.

The Faith Journey

"How does one become Catholic?" That's a question I have been asked hundreds of times, and I have given hundreds of different answers. For there are as many ways to become Catholic as there are individuals. When we talk about becoming Catholic, we are speaking about a person's faith journey, and each individual's journey is different. Consequently, there are many ways to become Catholic.

Catholics don't ordinarily talk much about their faith or their faith journey. As a catechist and teacher I have been in a fortunate position. I have heard many faith stories, those of Catholics and non-Catholics alike. And the more stories I hear, the more convinced I become that they are unique and personal journeys. God does not call all of us to the same journey. There are many roads to heaven. There are many paths to God.

But just as each individual is different, there are similarities. A surgeon beginning an operation knows that each person is unique but, at the same time, when the first incision is made, the surgeon expects to find in the location of various bodily organs some similarity between this person and previous patients. No operation is an entirely new adventure. A similar thing could be said about our faith journey: While each is unique, there are similar components.

Conversion

One day when I was driving from Dayton to Cincinnati using the "back way," the sky became overcast and I lost all sense of direction. After driving for several hours and seeing no sign of Cincinnati on the horizon, I stopped and asked a man working in his yard, "Excuse me, could you please point toward Cincinnati?" He gave me a strange look and pointed in the direction from which I had come. "Turn around," he said. "You're going the wrong way!"

If he had been speaking biblical Greek (which would have been a surprise), he would have told me, "*Metanoeite!*" In English, that is, "Repent; convert!"

"Turn around, you're going the wrong way" is the basic meaning of the biblical notion of repentance or conversion (see, for example, Mark 1:14-15). We turn from something in order to turn toward something different. And what do we turn *from* and turn *toward*? Saint Paul tells us we are to turn from *sarx*, that is, all that is selfish; all that seeks "me first" without considering the plan of God; all that is, in a word, sinful. We are to turn toward *pneuma*—that is, all that is life-giving and selfless, all that is generous, all that is Spirit-filled.

For some "converts" the journey begins with hearing about Jesus for the first time. I mean *really* hearing about Jesus: hearing in such a way as to experience in Jesus the visible revelation of the invisible God. For some people conversion happens suddenly, in a flash of light, like the conversion of Saint Paul recorded in Acts 9. But for most Catholics (and this has been my journey) conversion is more gradual. Some Christians are born again; Catholic Christians tend to be born again and again and again and again.

A multitude of different life events can cause one to begin the conversion process. Statistics show that the most common reason a person enters the Catholic Church is because that person has married a Catholic, is inspired by the faith of the spouse and motivated by the desire to raise the children in a common faith. (This is also the principal reason Catholics leave to join a different Church.) Others have fallen in love with a Catholic and want a "Catholic wedding."

But there are many reasons for beginning this journey: the good example of a close friend, a crisis—perhaps a sudden illness—in one's life. I know of a case where a person was simply driving down the street one day, passed a Catholic church, decided to go in, and while praying there decided to become Catholic. There is no explaining the movement of the Holy Spirit who, like the wind, blows where it will.

Inquiry
Usually a Catholic parish will sponsor an ongoing series of

"inquiry evenings," an hour or so of prayer, reflection and discussion for those who are curious about the Catholic Church and for those who are interested in becoming Catholic Christians. Some people find these meetings enjoyable and informative and participate in them for a number of years without actually ever having the desire to become Catholic. Others, through their association with this group and other movements of the Holy Spirit in their lives, feel the desire to take formal steps to join the Roman Catholic Church. The first formal step is to become a catechumen.

Catechumenate

Catechumen and *catechumenate* are ancient and traditional words which refer to the person and the process of becoming a Christian. The root meaning of the original word is "instruction." Catechesis or instruction is an important part of the catechumenate; a person who wants to become a Catholic will, naturally, want to know what Catholics know. The most important "thing" to know, of course, is to know Jesus. And *knowing* Jesus is different from knowing *about* Jesus. A person could know a lot about Jesus without knowing Jesus. The basic "textbook" for this instruction is the Sacred Scriptures. No book could be more helpful for knowing Jesus than the Bible.

Instruction, however, is only one component of the catechumenate process. There is also a "moral component" to the journey. As we come to know Jesus, we will want to act like Jesus. The journey is a journey of conversion, a process of turning around, turning from selfishness to Spirit-filled generosity. A person experiencing this conversion process frequently asks for a companion for the journey, a "spiritual director."

Most people will want to give this *inner* process of conversion an *external* expression: worship. Part of becoming a Catholic is worshiping together with Catholics, praying in a Catholic way. Catechumens will usually participate in Sunday Mass and be dismissed after the homily to continue their reflection on the word of God while the baptized share in Holy Communion.

This liturgical component of the catechumenate normally

leads to the fourth component: ministry. A person who knows Jesus will want to tell others about Jesus, both in word and deed. Often a beginner's enthusiasm needs to be held in check at this point, for effective ministry is usually accompanied by the mature faith of a long-practicing believer; but even a neophyte's journey will have a ministry component. Instruction, conversion, worship and ministry are the four components of the catechumenate.

The catechumenate has no fixed length. In some parishes the catechumenate extends from November until the beginning of Lent, but the parish attempts to respect the faith journey of the individual catechumen. Needless to say, this journey does not take place overnight. The path leads through a variety of spiritual seasons. There will be moments of insight and moments of doubt. There will be moments of fear and moments of great joy. There will be times of hesitancy and times of decision.

The Elect

There comes a point in this journey when one makes a decision to throw in one's lot with the Church and to be fully initiated into the Christian community. The catechumen chooses, "elects" the Church, and the Church chooses the individuals, who enter into a special group of catechumens, the elect, in a ceremony that takes place on the first Sunday of Lent, forty days before Easter.

This final period of preparation for Baptism we call Lent. Lent is a time for the catechumens to prepare for their Baptism, Confirmation and First Eucharist during the Easter Vigil. It is a time for those of us already baptized to encourage them, pray with them, and to rediscover the rich, ever powerful reality of our own Baptism.

On the first Sunday of Lent we hear of Jesus' temptations in the desert. The Gospel writers place these temptations after Jesus' Baptism. Moses led a people through the water (think Baptism) of the Red Sea into a desert (a place with no water) for forty years (Lent lasts forty days); there their identity as a

27

people was formed. Jesus comes up from the waters of Baptism in the Jordan and enters the desert for forty days; there his identity is revealed (a carpenter becomes the new Moses who forms a new people). This pattern is ours also: water (Baptism), desert (forty days of Lent), new identity. Egyptian slaves become a chosen people; a carpenter from Nazareth becomes Messiah; a new Moses forms a new people. Many parish churches use this desert theme in their decorations for Lent: absence of water, empty Baptismal font, no holy water, no flowers and plants that thrive on water.

On the first Sunday of Lent we see the elect of the parish state publicly their intention to be members of this Christian community by Baptism at Easter. They sign their lives away in the Book of the Elect. And we who are already Catholics ask ourselves: If we had it all to do over again, would we choose Baptism? Would we want to join this community? Do our lives contribute in some way to the attractiveness of this parish?

On the second Sunday we hear the story of the Transfiguration and see Jesus in his "Easter clothes." The elect will receive a white garment at their Baptism: they will come up from the baptismal pool dripping wet, dry off and put on their Easter clothes. This Gospel reminds us of our "Easter clothes": "As many of you as were baptized into Christ have clothed yourselves with Christ. There is no longer Jew or Greek, there is no longer slave or free, there is no longer male and female; for all of you are one in Christ Jesus" (Galatians 3:27-28).

Before we can put on that Easter garment (Christ), we must first take off our old clothes, the "isms" we renounced at Baptism: racism, sexism, militarism, nationalism. We can no longer make decisions based on false dichotomies of "Jew or Greek, slave or free, male or female."

On the third Sunday we find Jesus at a well in Samaria, thirsting. A woman asks for "living water." She is converted and believes in Jesus, and she hastens to make disciples of others. She is a model for each of the baptized, who have received the water that only Jesus can give. As the catechumens withdraw into their desert space during Lent, they ask themselves what they are thirsty for. They ask what cares and worries occupy their minds and their time. Are these the same things Jesus is thirsting for? Sometimes we need actual physical fasting from certain foods or drinks to recognize our true hungers and thirsts.

Several times during Lent we see those preparing for Baptism come forward during the Mass to be questioned about their progress, strengthened with the Oil of Catechumens and prayed over by the community, their catechists and godparents.

The Gospel of the Fourth Sunday of Lent reminds us of an ancient name for Christian Baptism, "illumination." We hear the story of the man born blind, walking in darkness until he meets Jesus. Jesus tells him: " 'Go, wash in the pool of Siloam' (which means Sent). Then he went and washed and came back able to see" (John 9:7).

The elect want to be washed—baptized—in Christ, the One who has been sent. They want to be illumined and by faith to see things in a new way. We who are already baptized pray for the elect. We ask ourselves if we actually do see things differently than our non-Christian neighbors. Does hearing the Gospel at Mass Sunday after Sunday make a difference in the way we think about poverty, health care, war, drugs? Do we see people as they are or only for what they can do for us? Do we let our eyes see images that make us so greedy for possessions or sex or power that we cannot hear the word of God? In our desert place we pray for the gift of true sight: to see as God sees.

As Lent comes to a close and the night for initiation approaches, the story of Lazarus, called forth from the tomb and given new life (Fifth Sunday), is a vivid image of what will happen to the elect. They will die to sin, be buried with Christ and will be called forth from the tomb and given new life. They will promise to "reject sin so as to live in the freedom of God's children" (*Rite of Christian Initiation of Adults*). And we ask ourselves if we are really free. In the tomb Lazarus was bound with strips of cloth. What memories or addictions bind us and keep us from being truly free?

Initiation: What Does It Look Like?

It is the Saturday night before Easter. Jesus, Lent, Church, Baptism, Confirmation, Eucharist all come together in this holy night. A vigil is a time to wait and watch. We wait with the catechumens. We wait with generations of those who waited for Christ to come from the tomb.

The ceremony begins after nightfall. We sit around a blazing fire and tell the stories which give meaning to the sacraments of initiation: the creation story (life emerging from water), the flood (Noah and his family saved by water), Abraham called to sacrifice Isaac (our sacrificing all to follow Christ). Finally we hear Paul assure us that if we have died with Christ in Baptism we will surely rise with him. We shout forth our alleluia—a word that is fresh and new as we have not used it during these forty days of Lent. And with the alleluia on our lips we hear the Gospel proclamation of Christ's Resurrection. It is the proclamation of our own resurrection.

The elect come forward and we pray that what happened to Christ may happen to them. We watch as they go down into the tomb with Jesus, emerge dripping wet with new life and are sealed with the chrism of salvation—confirmed.

The vigil comes to its climax with the celebration of the Eucharist. We join the newly initiated and those initiated last year and years ago, and we break our Lenten fast with the new food of the Kingdom, Holy Communion. The elect have celebrated the sacraments of Baptism, Confirmation, Eucharist. They have been initiated. They have passed from the Order of Catechumens to the Order of Faithful.

Later we will consider in detail the meaning of the Eucharist and then take a "walk through the Mass." But before concluding this present chapter, we will look at the meaning of Baptism and Confirmation.

Initiation: What Does It Mean?

In the early Church it was common usage to speak of the entire process described above—the catechumenate, Lent, the Vigil, the sacraments of Baptism, Confirmation, Eucharist—as Baptism. This usage is common again today. When I speak of Baptism in the following paragraphs I am including this whole process.

It is easy to describe what the ceremonies of Baptism look like; it is more difficult to say what they mean. I have found that the best way to understand what Baptism means is to listen carefully to the images and metaphors those who have been baptized use to describe their experience. Many of these metaphors are recorded for us in the Christian Scriptures.

Baptism is being born again. As Jesus said to Nicodemus, " 'Very truly, I tell you, no one can see the kingdom of God without being born from above.' Nicodemus said to him, 'How can anyone be born after growing old? Can one enter a second time into the mother's womb and be born?' " (John 3:3-4). Yet being born again is the experience of those emerging from the waters of Baptism. We come forth from the waters of our mother's womb and are born into a human family, loved by our parents and receiving their family name. We come forth from the womb of Baptism born of God into the family of the Church filled with the Spirit of love and receive the family name: Christian.

Baptism is dying. "Do you not know that all of us who have been baptized into Christ Jesus were baptized into his death? Therefore we have been buried with him by baptism into death, so that, just as Christ was raised from the dead by the glory of the Father, so we too might walk in newness of life" (Romans 6:3-4). In Baptism we go down into the tomb. We are buried with Christ. We die to *sarx* (selfishness and sin) so that the Spirit (*pneuma*) of Christ may be born in us.

Baptism is seeing things in a new light. The Pharisees asked the man who had been blind from birth "how he had received his sight. He said to them, 'He put mud on my eyes. Then I washed, and now I see' " (John 9:15). Jesus, the light of the world, instructs those who walk in the darkness of sin to go and wash (to be baptized) in Siloam (in Christ, the one who has been sent into the world). We emerge from the waters of Baptism and see things in a new light. We see things with God's eyes. We see a world where we are no longer alone but where we are interconnected with every other creature. We see a world where we are no longer left to ourselves but where we are loved and empowered by the Spirit of God.

Baptism is being adopted to a new family—the family of God. "It is that very Spirit bearing witness with our spirit that we are children of God, and if children, then heirs, heirs of God and joint heirs with Christ—if, in fact, we suffer with him so that we may also be glorified with him" (Romans 8:16-17). At our natural birth, we are born from our mother's womb and are embraced as her child. At Baptism, we are born from the womb of the Church and become Christian. Baptism is the voice of the Parent's love. When we are loved, we are empowered to grow, to love, to perform generous deeds. Jesus, the carpenter of Nazareth, entered the Jordan at his baptism. "And a voice from heaven said, 'This is my Son, the Beloved, with whom I am well pleased' " (Matthew 3:17). Jesus emerged from the river, empowered by that love, to save the world.

Confirmation

The externals of Christian initiation are influenced by the customs and practices of second- and third-century Roman culture, in which our rites were formed and developed. In Roman times the body was rubbed with oil after bathing to strengthen and moisturize it. Similarly, the water bath of Baptism was complemented by a postbaptismal anointing, which we have come to call Confirmation. In the early days of the Church we do not find much reference to Confirmation as a sacrament, for it was seen as an integral part of the process of Baptism. Baptism is being cleansed of sin; Confirmation is being filled with grace. Baptism is dying with Christ; Confirmation is rising to new life.

In the third and fourth centuries the Church expanded rapidly and our understanding of Christian ministry changed. In some countries the postbaptismal anointing by the bishop began to be separated from the water bath when the latter rite was presided over by a minister other than the local bishop. When Confirmation was celebrated later, apart from Baptism,

Christians began to speak of it as a separate sacrament.

The Second Vatican Council restored our understanding of the unity of the sacraments of Christian initiation. Today when people other than infants are initiated into the Church, they experience Baptism, Confirmation and Eucharist in one ritual event. That experience is our source for understanding Baptism and Confirmation. The meaning of Confirmation is found in this initiation event.

The Baptism of Infants

Some Christian Churches do not believe that infants should be baptized. They feel that Baptism requires a personal decision, that parents should wait and let the child decide whether to be baptized or not. We Catholics, however, have a long history of baptizing infants.

The reasons given for this practice have varied during different periods of our history. There was a time when Catholic parents were urged with threats about limbo to have their infants baptized. But the parents I know today are not very moved by this line of reasoning. They somehow intuitively know that God loves their infant. When they look into the face of their newborn baby and feel the love they have for it, they know deep in their heart that God loves this innocent child and has created it for eternal happiness.

Why then baptize an infant? There are many reasons for infant Baptism, including original sin, the fallen human condition. I will focus here on one that is important to all of us, even those whose Church does not follow this practice.

When I celebrate the Baptism of an infant and see the baby held lovingly in its parents' arms, I receive a sacrament of the mystery of God. I and the whole congregation witnessing this event get a glimpse of who God is for us. In Mark's Gospel people were bringing children to Jesus so that he could bless them, and the disciples tried to keep the children away. "But when Jesus saw this he was indignant and said to them, 'Let the little children come to me; do not stop them; for it is to such as these that the kingdom of God belongs. Truly I tell you, whoever does not receive the kingdom of God as a little child will never enter it' " (see Mark 10:13-16).

Here in America we are proud to live in a land of personal freedom and individual responsibility. We each strive to be all that we can be. In this context we may wonder what words of Jesus about accepting the rule of God like a child could mean. Surely Jesus doesn't want us to remain forever in diapers, speechless and helpless! Infant Baptism helps me understand these words of Jesus. Infant Baptism gives us an experience of who we are before God: radically dependent on our loving Parent. This is our most honest, deepest and truest stance before God. "Amen, I say to you, whoever does not accept the rule of God like a little child will not enter it" is an image of the relationship between the human race and its Creator. We receive a sacrament of God's rule.

Baptism in Daily Living

I saw Niagara Falls once, and it was very beautiful. I remember the event; I am glad I was there. Baptism was also an event in my past life, but Baptism is not *just* a past event. Once Baptism is experienced, its effects remain with us forever.

Many of my friends are married, but the marriage is not merely a *past event*—something they did on a Saturday afternoon long ago. What they did on that occasion has influenced all their decisions since. The promises that I made long ago at my Baptism (or in my case, the promises which my parents made for me, for I was baptized as an infant) need to be renewed and strengthened each day of my life, just as the vows that a husband and wife make to each other on their wedding day must be daily renewed and strengthened if the marriage is to grow and mature.

And what did I promise on that day? I promised that I would renounce Satan: that I would "reject the glamour of evil/and refuse to be mastered by sin" (*Rite of Baptism*). To turn from sin I must know what sins I face.

And when I promised to reject sin, what did I receive in return? According to Paul's Letter to the Colossians, we have clothed ourselves

with the new self, which is being renewed in
knowledge according to the image of its creator. In
that renewal there is no longer Greek and Jew,
circumcised and uncircumcised, barbarian, Scythian,
slave and free; but Christ is all in all!

As God's chosen ones, holy and beloved, clothe
yourselves with compassion, kindness, humility,
meekness, and patience. Bear with one another, if
anyone has a complaint against another, forgive each
other; just as the Lord has forgiven you, so you also
must forgive. Above all, clothe yourselves with love,
which binds everything together in perfect harmony
(Colossians 3:10-14).

FOR PRAYER

Jesus, help me to know you;
    help me to see the road I am to follow
    in coming to you.
Enlighten me
    so that I may know the path you want me to follow.
Strengthen me
    so that I may choose that path
    and embrace it with love.

Loving God,
I have been/will be baptized
    into the passion, death and resurrection of your Son.
Help me to live that risen life.
Each day I wish to renew the promises of my Baptism.
I wish to die to sin and especially to _____.
Help me to grow in the risen life of Christ, especially
    by_____.

FOR REFLECTION AND DISCUSSION

1) Close your eyes and say "Baptism." With an imaginary camera take a picture of your mental image of Baptism. Develop the picture and hold it in your hand to examine it. Who is being baptized in this picture, an adult or an infant? How many people are present? How much water is there in the picture? How much oil? How much bread and wine?

2) If you are not Catholic, does your Church practice the rite of Confirmation? Why or why not?

3) Should infants be baptized? Why or why not?

FOR FURTHER INFORMATION

Regis Duffy, *On Becoming a Catholic: The Challenge of Christian Initiation*. San Francisco: Harper and Row Publishers, 1984.

Carol Luebering, *What Do You Ask for Your Child? Exploring the Reasons for Baptism*. Cincinnati: St. Anthony Messenger Press, 1979.

Kenan Osborne, *The Christian Sacraments of Initiation: Baptism, Confirmation, Eucharist*. New York: Paulist Press, 1987.

Catechism of the Catholic Church, "The Sacraments of Christian Initiation" (#1212-1324).

CHAPTER THREE

A House for the Church:
A Tour

Margaret and Joe, members of our parish, recently asked me: "Father, some of the non-Catholic friends we invited to our daughter's wedding asked us about the things they saw in our church. 'Why do you have a bowl of water at the door?' 'Why are there pictures of Christ with little numbers under them around the walls?' We weren't able to give them many good answers! We knew about the stations and could answer some of their questions, but most of these things we just grew up with. We never really questioned why they are there or where they came from. What can we tell our friends when they ask us these things?"

In this chapter we will take a tour of a Catholic church and answer some of these questions. Your church may not look exactly like the one we tour in this article. The church *building* is a home for the Church, the *people*, the parish family. I don't expect any two of my friends to furnish their homes in exactly the same way. Some like modern, others the more traditional. We can expect differences in our church buildings, too.

I would never thoughtlessly criticize a friend's home, for I know that the home is an expression of my friend's personality and values. To criticize the home is to criticize the friend! Similarly, I want to be very careful in our tour of a Catholic church, for the church building is an expression of the personality and values, the Catholic faith of the parish family that worships there. To criticize their church building is to criticize not their taste, but their faith.

Many of the explanations and comments I will make on our tour I have taken from a little book published by the American bishops, *Environment and Art in Catholic Worship*.

Baptism: The Door

One of the first things we see when we enter the *narthex* or vestibule of a Catholic church is a pool of water. Baptism is the "door" to the Church, the way by which we enter Christ's family. The baptismal pool or font at the door of the Church reminds Catholics that every time they come to Eucharist they come through Baptism. They dip their hand in the water and mark themselves anew with that sign in which they were baptized, the Sign of the Cross. In many churches a bowl of water, a holy water font, at each door substitutes for the baptismal pool.

Standing by the baptismal pool is a large candle, the paschal or Easter candle. At the Vigil on the eve of Easter Sunday this candle impregnated the waters of the baptismal pool as the Church prayed that the Holy Spirit unseal this font, the womb of new life for the Church. As the candle was placed in the water we prayed:

> May all who are buried with Christ
>   in the death of baptism
>   rise also with him to newness of life.
> (Blessing of Water at the Easter Vigil)

This prayer takes on special meaning at funerals, when this water is sprinkled on the casket as it arrives at the church door.

Also in the baptismal area, you will see a niche in the wall or a little chest, the ambry, which contains three vessels of oil: the Oil of Catechumens, which is used to bless and strengthen those preparing for Baptism; the Oil of the Sick, with which the priest strengthens and heals those who are joined with the suffering Christ in serious illness; and the Sacred Chrism, which is used in celebrating the sacraments of Baptism, Confirmation and Holy Orders. The word *Christ* means "anointed." When one is anointed with holy oil it is a sign of a special relationship with Christ and of the presence of the Anointed One.

In more recently constructed churches, you will also see in this baptismal area a door leading to the reconciliation chapel, a small room designed for the celebration of the Sacrament of Reconciliation (confession). The reconciliation chapel is located in the baptismal area because of the historical relation between these two sacraments: The Sacrament of Penance developed from the need to reconcile Christians who were not faithful to their baptismal promises and who had separated themselves from the community by their sins, as we will see in Chapter Six.

In some churches you will see one or more confessionals, small "rooms" built out from the wall of the church. Each contains a place for the confessor to sit, separated by a screen or grill from a place for the penitent to kneel and confess his or her sins.

Confessionals appeared in Catholic churches during the sixteenth century and were a common feature of churches until just recently. The current ritual for the individual celebration of the sacrament offers the penitent a choice between speaking face-to-face with the priest or the anonymity provided by the confessional screen; this option has necessitated the remodeling of confessionals in some churches and the construction of reconciliation chapels in others.

The Church: God's Assembly

Entering the church proper, the *nave* (from the Latin word for "boat"), we find ourselves in a large assembly room. If we are taking our tour at a time when the liturgy is not being celebrated and no people are present, the space may look a little strange, but that is normal. The space only looks right when it is functioning. Visiting an empty church is something like visiting an amusement park during the winter when it is closed. We can imagine what the park would look like with lights flashing and music playing and children running through crowds of happy people, but the park needs the people and the activity to look right. Similarly, the nave of the church "needs an assembly of people to complete it" (*Environment and Art in Catholic Worship*, #24). It will only look "right" when it is actually functioning as a space for God's people at prayer.

Perhaps the greatest difference between a church and almost all other large public assembly areas we are used to visiting (theaters, cinemas, opera houses, sports arenas) is that in the church there is no "stage." Most large public spaces have a place where the action takes place and a place for the spectators or audience. At Mass there is no "audience"; consequently the entire space within the church has a special unity. *Environment and Art in Catholic Worship* states:

> Special attention must be given to the unity of the entire liturgical space. Before considering the distinction of roles within the liturgy, the space should communicate an integrity (a sense of oneness, of wholeness) and a sense of being the gathering place of the initiated community. Within that one space there are different areas corresponding to different roles and functions, but the wholeness of the total space should be strikingly evident. (#53)

The nave is usually filled with benches, or pews (from the Greek *podion*, the place where the emperor and other distinguished persons sat in the arena. Many of the names of things we will see on our tour come from the Greek or Latin names for these objects.).

Catholics expect to find pews in a church; they are surprised when they enter one of the older churches of Europe and find no pews or fixed seating! The absence of pews in older churches is a reminder that the principal posture for Catholic worship is *standing*. We stand in the presence of one we wish to honor and to serve, just as the priest stands at the altar during Mass. Standing is a mark of reverence and readiness.

Pews and fixed seating entered the church at about the same time western culture discovered the printing press; people in church began to "line up" like lines on a printed page to hear the word of God read to them from a printed book. At the time of the Reformation, pews enabled the congregation to sit and listen to the sermon, which often lasted several hours.

Fixed pews reinforced the image of the congregation as "listeners"—like the audience in an auditorium (from *audire*,

Latin for "to listen"). As we have seen, we are present as doers, actively engaged in the liturgical action, not merely as listeners.

Some new churches today do not have fixed pews but use individual chairs. A more flexible seating arrangement encourages a more active and participatory liturgy. Church architects are "striving for a seating pattern and furniture that do not constrict people but encourage them to move about when it is appropriate" (*Environment and Art in Catholic Worship*, #68).

In the thirteenth century, when Catholics no longer received Holy Communion frequently and the high point of the Mass was *looking* at the sacred Host after the Consecration, Christians began to kneel at this point in the Mass. As the practice of kneeling was extended, kneeling benches were introduced, often attached to the backs of the chairs or pews. You still see kneelers in many churches today, although the more traditional position of standing during worship is once more gaining favor with the faithful.

Around the walls of many churches you will find the Way of the Cross: pictures (numbered from one to fourteen) of incidents in Jesus' last journey from Pilate's house, where he was condemned to death, to his entombment. From an early date pilgrims to the Holy Land would follow in the footsteps of Jesus on his way to Calvary. In the later Middle Ages the devotional Way of the Cross was made popular, especially by the Franciscans, to enable those who could not afford the rigors and expense of a long pilgrimage to participate in Jesus' passion in their own villages. The faithful go to each of the stations and meditate on an event of the Passion.

The movement around the church also enables us to take possession of this sacred space and claim it as our own. The church, however, is primarily a place for our public worship; our personal devotions should not distract from its principal function.

Focus of the Sacred Action

From wherever we stand in the church, our attention is drawn to the focal area of the liturgical action and to the three pieces of furniture we find there: the presider's chair, the lectern and the altar. Formerly this area was called the sanctuary (Latin *sanctus*, "holy"). But we must be careful not to let *sanctuary* imply that this is the only holy area, for indeed the entire church, the entire assembly area, is a holy place.

In the front of the assembly area we find a special seat for the one presiding and leading the assembly. In the principal church of a diocese, this chair, the *cathedra* (from the Greek word for "chair") gives a name to the entire building, *cathedral*. Each church will have a presider's chair or bench and seating for the other ministers. This seating is arranged so that the ministers are "clearly part of the one assembly, yet conveniently situated for the exercise of their respective offices" (*Environment and Art in Catholic Worship*, #70).

Also in this focus area we see a reading stand. Once it was called the *ambo* (from the Latin word for *both* because there were two of them, one for the Epistle and one for the Gospel). After the fourteenth century the ambo was replaced by a pulpit (Latin *pulpitum*, a raised platform for speaking). Today the pulpit is usually replaced by a lectern (Latin *legere*, "to read"), from which we proclaim the word of God and upon which is placed the lectionary, the book of readings from Scripture. Some churches will also have an *Evangeliary*, a book containing the Gospels (Greek, *euaggelion*, "gospel"). The size, design and binding of these books "are a significant part of the liturgical environment" (*Environment and Art in Catholic Worship*, #91). Preaching can be done from the lectern, the chair or elsewhere.

In some churches you may see a second, very simple lectern, which is used by the song leader and reader of the announcements. The main ambo or lectern "represents the dignity and uniqueness of the word of God" (*Environment and Art in Catholic Worship*, #74) and is used only for that purpose.

Ritual Clothing and Furniture

Vestments, the special ritual clothing worn by those who lead the assembly in prayer, are "an appropriate symbol of their service" (*Environment and Art in Catholic Worship*, #93) and add their own element of beauty to the celebration. The priest wears a long white garment, an alb (from *albus*, Latin for white) and over it a chasuble (from the Latin for "little house").

Today these garments look quite different from ordinary street clothing; originally this was not the case. The alb and chasuble were ordinary garments in the Greco-Roman world. Around the house both men and women wore an alb, a long, loose-fitting garment; when going out in public they put on a more ornate garment, a chasuble, over the alb. If you attended Mass in fourth-century Rome, the leader of the liturgical assembly would be dressed in much the same way as the priest today vests for Sunday Mass. But at that time, *everyone* in the church would be wearing an alb and chasuble!

Since the ninth century the priest has also worn a stole, a long piece of cloth about four inches wide draped around the neck. The origin and meaning of this vestment is lost in history.

The altar is the holy table upon which we celebrate the Lord's Supper. It functions as both altar of sacrifice and banquet table, for the Eucharist is both "a memorial of Christ's death and resurrection," and "a paschal banquet in which Christ is eaten, the heart is filled with grace, and a pledge of future glory given to us" (*Constitution on the Liturgy*, #47). No ordinary table would be able to bear the weight of these symbolic functions; that is why this table "should be the most noble, the most beautifully designed and constructed table the community can provide" (*Environment and Art in Catholic Worship*, #71)

When the Liturgy of the Eucharist is celebrated the table is covered with an altar cloth or tablecloth. On the altar is placed the bread and wine for Mass. The bread is on a bread plate or paten (from *patella*, meaning "platter," "plate") and the wine is poured into a chalice (from *calix*, the Latin word for "cup" or "goblet").

We also find in this area a cross or crucifix. This may be a

43

processional cross with a floor stand or a cross hanging from the ceiling or on the wall. In the cross we see the basic symbol of any Christian liturgical celebration; in the Paschal Mystery of Christ we find our own image as a Christian community.

The Tabernacle

When I was a child, the climax of a tour of a Catholic church would have been the tabernacle (*tabernaculum*, Latin for "tent"), the "little house" in which the Blessed Sacrament was kept. The tabernacle was the first thing I looked for upon entering a church. The little golden door on the high altar with a red lamp burning before it was the sure sign that I was in a *Catholic* church.

Today, with increasing frequency, we will not find a tabernacle on our tour of the assembly area of a Catholic church. More has changed than just rearranging furniture: There has been a major change in our understanding of the Eucharist. This change has upset not a few Catholics; they do not like liturgists and architects tampering with their faith, particularly their faith in the Lord's real presence in the Eucharist.

The reasons—the very important and serious reasons—for taking the tabernacle from the altar in the sanctuary area and placing it in its own eucharistic chapel are explained in the Bishops' statement on the environment for worship:

> The *celebration* of the eucharist is the focus of the normal Sunday assembly. As such, the major space of a church is designed for this *action*. Beyond the celebration of the eucharist, the Church has had a most ancient tradition of reserving the eucharistic bread. The purpose of this reservation is to bring communion to the sick and to be the object of private devotion. Most appropriately, this reservation should be designated in a space designed for individual devotion. A room or chapel specifically designed and separate from the major space is important so that no confusion

44

can take place between the celebration of the eucharist and reservation. Active and static aspects of the same reality cannot claim the same human attention at the same time. Having the eucharist reserved in a place apart does not mean it has been relegated to a secondary place of no importance. Rather, a space carefully designed and appointed can give proper attention to the reserved sacrament. (*Environment and Art in Catholic Worship*, #78)

A lamp, often a red votive candle or sanctuary lamp burning before the tabernacle, has traditionally served Catholics as the sign that the consecrated bread is present there. Other candles will be found in both devotional areas and the assembly area of the Church. Once they were primarily used to give light for reading the Scriptures and celebrating the sacred action. Now that churches are fitted with electrical lighting, the symbolic function of the candles remains: the beautiful quality of candlelight. The candle consumes itself in service of the sacred mysteries. Sometimes Catholics will light a votive candle in front of a statue or shrine as a reminder that their prayers continue even after they leave the church.

Statues

Another high point in a tour of a Catholic church was often the reredos (from *arrere*, "behind," and *dos*, "back"), the statues and paintings on the back of the altar together with their beautiful and elaborately carved shrines. This extension of the altar is what most Catholics once meant when they spoke of the altar, rather than the table itself. These altars with reredos were often objects of great beauty, the focal point of the assembly area and the pride of the parish.

In churches built today we usually do not see a reredos. In older churches which have been recently remodeled, the removal of statues and the "high altar" has caused even more protest from Catholics than the removal of the tabernacle. Understandably, the reasons for these changes must be as

45

serious as the pain they have caused.

In the early Middle Ages a greater stress began to be placed on the sacredness of the Mass and the otherworldly character of the mysteries. Holy Communion was received only by the clergy. The altar gradually moved away from the assembly of the faithful to the rear of the choir and was placed against the back wall. The back wall itself began to have a special significance. The wall had been ornamented from early times, often with a painting of the cross, the Lamb of God, the Good Shepherd or the glorified Christ. People began to place these paintings on the altar itself; then the altar was extended back and up to form the reredos. Statues appeared on this extension of the altar: first the crucifixion, then the martyr whose relics were under the altar or the saint in whose honor the church was dedicated; later other saints were added.

The statues and paintings of the saints aided the devotion of the faithful at a time when active participation in the liturgical action was reserved to the clergy. The statues placed us in union with heroic Christians of other times and places. The saints were intercessors for particular favors and blessings.

At the time of the Reformation, many Protestant Churches removed these decorations so that the word of God could be heard more clearly. Excessive decoration can be a hindrance to effective preaching. As the American playwright Thornton Wilder said of his minimal staging for his plays: "If the eye sees too much, the ear doesn't really listen."

Because the liturgy was in a language most people did not understand, Catholics were not as concerned about the ear and continued to create a visual feast for the eye. This changed when the Second Vatican Council allowed the liturgy in our own language so that we could hear the Scriptures and understand the prayers and proclaim our faith in songs and acclamations. Today Catholics are beginning to look for a balance: seeing, hearing, doing. One sign of our new interest in hearing is our increasing concern for good preaching and quality homilies.

We will not strengthen the ear by starving the eye! There is no movement to remove statues and decoration simply to make our churches bare and plain. Quite the contrary. To quote again the bishops' statement on the environment: "In a world dominated by science and technology, liturgy's quest for the beautiful is a particularly necessary contribution to full and balanced human life" (*Environment and Art in Catholic Worship*, #34). Statues and beautiful objects of art, banners and flowers will always be an important part of the environment for our worship.

One of the historical functions of stained glass windows, in addition to bathing the assembly area with their beautiful light, was to illustrate the stories of the Bible for those who could not read or afford expensive manuscripts. (The thirteenth century windows of the Sainte Chapelle in Paris contain 1,134 illustrations from the Bible!) But such objects do not merely teach; they are not history lessons. Their artistic beauty reveals to us something of the beauty of God and God's dreams for us. Surrounded by created, artistic beauty we are led to the vision of Uncreated Beauty, God. Our liturgical renewal has helped us become more aware that the principal function of the church is to house our common worship. Objects which compete with that purpose are out of place. Images in painting or sculpture "must take into account the current renewed emphasis on the action of the assembly. If instead of serving and aiding that action, they threaten it or compete with it, then they are unsuitable" (*Environment and Art in Catholic Worship*, #98).

Today the principal "decoration," the most treasured possession of a church is the worshiping community. That is why the church "needs an assembly of people to complete it" (*Environment and Art in Catholic Worship*, #24). Images and the faces of the saints have always aided our worship. Today, when the assembly space is designed to enable us to see the other members of the congregation, we take encouragement from the faces of the living saints, the heroes and heroines who carry the message of the Eucharist out into our world and our time.

Our tour has led us through a great variety of Catholic churches: some with many statues and some with none; through churches with golden altars and ceilings and those with wooden altars and plaster ceilings. But as in the homes of my friends, which vary with their wealth and taste, the important thing is

47

the warmth, hospitality and friendship I experience there. The principal beauty of the Catholic church is the hospitality of its assembly, the eagerness with which they hear the word of God, the devotion with which they share the Eucharist and the love they take forth to transform the earth.

FOR PRAYER

How lovely is your dwelling place,
    O LORD of hosts!
My soul longs, indeed it faints
    for the courts of the LORD;
my heart and my flesh sing for joy
    to the living God. (Psalm 84:1-2)

Loving Jesus, you yourself are the "living stone,
though rejected by mortals
yet chosen and precious in God's sight...."
Let me be built "into a spiritual house
to be a holy priesthood,
and offer spiritual sacrifices acceptable to God...."
(see 1 Peter 2:4-5)

One thing I asked of the LORD,
    that will I seek after:
to live in the house of the LORD
    all the days of my life,
to behold the beauty of the LORD,
    and to inquire in his temple. (Psalm 27:4)

FOR REFLECTION AND DISCUSSION

1) What is the most beautiful church you have ever seen? Why?

2) How does the shape and decoration of the Catholic church described here compare with the church you usually attend?

3) Do you believe that money spent on churches and beautiful vestments is well spent? Or could this money be better used to serve the poor?

FOR FURTHER INFORMATION

Bishops' Committee on the Liturgy, *Environment and Art in Catholic Worship*. Washington, D.C.: Office of Publishing and Promotion Services, United States Catholic Conference, 1978.

Bishops' Committee on the Liturgy, *Liturgical Music Today*. Washington, D.C.: Office of Publishing and Promotion Services, United States Catholic Conference, 1982.

Bishops' Committee on the Liturgy, *Music in Catholic Worship*, Revised Edition. Washington, D.C.: Office of Publishing and Promotion Services, United States Catholic Conference, 1983.

Thomas Simons and James Fitzpatrick, *The Ministry of Liturgical Environment*. Collegeville, Minn.: The Liturgical Press, 1984.

Catechism of the Catholic Church, "Celebrating the Church's Liturgy" (#1135-1199); "Truth, Beauty, and Sacred Art" (#2500-2513).

CHAPTER FOUR

The First Sacrament:
Eucharist

The Eucharist should really be Chapter One! The Eucharist is the first sacrament. It is the first sacrament in the sense that it is the principal sacrament, the principal manifestation of Jesus Christ, the root and source of all the sacraments. Furthermore, Eucharist is the *model* of all the other sacraments; it says all that the other sacraments can say. Eucharist is the sacrament that, in a most perfect way, makes present and models the Church. It is not only *one* of the seven sacraments, it is *the* sacrament—for it contains all that we are, all that the Church is, all that Jesus says of God.

In Chapter Two we walked in the footsteps of one coming to Eucharist for the first time. We spoke of the meaning of the first rites of the initiation process: the catechumenate, Baptism and Confirmation. In this chapter we will consider the meaning of the Eucharist, the culminating sacrament of Christian initiation.

In the sacraments of initiation we are born again into that new life which is the life of Christ himself. As Catholic Christians we realize the need to grow and mature in this Christ life. The water bath (Baptism) and the anointing (Confirmation) are never repeated. We continue to renew the promises of our Baptism and to be strengthened in their resolve by the sacrament of Eucharist. Eucharist is the repeatable part of Christian initiation.

What Does It Mean?

What does Eucharist mean? I wish I could answer that

question! I thought that I knew what Eucharist was when I received my First Communion at the age of seven. I thought that I knew what Eucharist was when I was ordained a priest in 1966. Each year I teach courses on the Eucharist at a graduate school of theology, and each year I am amazed at how much I learn. We can never understand Eucharist fully.

While it may be impossible to understand the Eucharist fully, I have become convinced that the road to understanding leads through three events or images: Good Friday, Holy Thursday and Easter Sunday.

Christian Churches differ in the emphasis they give to these images with regard to their understanding of the Eucharist. Some put the primary emphasis on Holy Thursday and speak of celebrating "the Lord's Supper." Many Catholic Christians think of the Eucharist primarily in terms of Good Friday and speak of "the Holy Sacrifice of the Mass." I have come to believe that balance is the key.

Good Friday: The Holy Sacrifice of the Mass

Good Friday was the main image which shaped my eucharistic devotion when I was a child. When I entered my parish church in Wichita, Kansas, the first thing I saw was a larger-than-life-size crucifix hanging over the altar. I knew that being at Mass was like kneeling at the foot of Jesus' cross on Calvary with the Virgin Mary and Saint John. My silent reverence at Mass reflected their reverence at the death of Jesus. In grade school I learned from my *Baltimore Catechism* that the Mass was "the sacrifice of the New Law in which Christ, through the ministry of the priest, offers himself to God in an unbloody manner under the appearances of bread and wine." Even though I did not understand the full meaning of some of these words, the mention of sacrifice, priest, offering and blood brought to my mind the image of Good Friday; I permanently associated the Eucharist with Jesus' death on the cross.

I never thought much about the meal aspect of the Mass (the Holy Thursday image) when I was a child. This may seem strange today, when nearly everyone receives Holy

Communion at Sunday Mass. In the 1940's this was not the case; very few people received Holy Communion at Mass. And because I understood the Mass in terms of Good Friday, going to Communion was not an issue. After all, no one went to Communion on that first Good Friday! I expressed my devotion to the Eucharist by kneeling at the foot of the cross, gazing at the sacrifice of Jesus, expressing my gratitude for so great a love and being sorry for my sins, which caused such great suffering.

The image of Good Friday remains an essential element of the Catholic understanding of Eucharist. But while it is essential, it is not enough. An adequate understanding of the Eucharist involves not only Good Friday, but also Holy Thursday and Easter Sunday.

Holy Thursday: The Lord's Supper

During the 1950's, when more and more people began to receive Communion at Mass, Holy Thursday gradually began to play a larger role in our understanding of the Eucharist. During the 1970's the parish with which I celebrated the Eucharist began to use bread in place of hosts at Mass, bread that looked and tasted like "real" bread. People began to take Holy Communion in their hands and to drink from the cup. Mass began to look more like a meal. Altars began to look more like tables. The songs and prayers of the Mass spoke openly about eating and drinking, about meals, suppers and banquets.

All of these things caused the image of Holy Thursday to be added to the image of Good Friday in helping Catholics understand the Eucharist. My own devotion began to take on a more joyful tone. I began to speak of "celebrating the Eucharist" rather than "going to Mass." To the image of kneeling at the foot of the cross I added the image of sitting with Christ and the saints at the heavenly banquet, listening to his words, sharing the consecrated bread and wine.

And now, as I grow older and continue to reflect on the meaning of the Eucharist, I see how the image of Easter Sunday is also essential for an adequate understanding of the Eucharist.

Easter Sunday: The Body of Christ

Saint Paul realized from the moment of his conversion that the risen Christ was so identified with the baptized that to persecute Christians was to persecute Christ. Not just once, but three times Paul's experience is described in the Acts of the Apostles. In Acts 9 we see Saul (not yet Saint Paul) terrorizing the followers of Jesus when suddenly one day, on the road to Damascus, "He fell to the ground and heard a voice saying to him, 'Saul, Saul, why do you persecute me?' He asked, 'Who are you, Lord?' The reply came, 'I am Jesus, whom you are persecuting'" (Acts 9:4-5).

Later Paul himself retells the incident: "I fell to the ground and heard a voice saying to me, 'Saul, Saul, why are you persecuting me?' I answered, 'Who are you, Lord?' Then he said to me, "'I am Jesus of Nazareth whom you are persecuting'" (Acts 22:7-8). Paul tells the story again in Acts 26: "I am Jesus whom you are persecuting" (26:15b). The experience revealed to Paul that Christ cannot be separated from his members. The risen Lord is so united to the Christian that what we do to one another, we do to Christ. The eucharistic Body of Christ is *our* body.

This was the very point at issue in the First Letter to the Corinthians, the earliest written account we have of the Last Supper (from about the year 50 C.E.). Paul angrily voices his concern to the Corinthians about the way they understand the Eucharist:

> [W]hen you come together, it is not for the better but for the worse. For, to begin with, when you come together as a church, I hear that there are divisions among you; and to some extent I believe it.... When you come together, it is not really to eat the Lord's supper. For when the time comes to eat, each of you goes ahead with your own supper, and one goes hungry and another becomes drunk. What! Do you not have homes to eat and drink in? Or do you show contempt for the church of God and humiliate those who have nothing? What should I say to you? Should I

commend you? In this matter I do not commend you!
(1 Corinthians 11:17-18, 20-22)

Paul reproaches the Corinthians for celebrating the Eucharist
without recognizing the Body of Christ: the poor who go
hungry while the rich get drunk. His criticism of their
eucharistic devotion is not directed toward the songs they were
singing or the vestments they were wearing or whether they
received Communion standing up or kneeling down or any of
the other issues that disturb some Catholics today. The issue
was much more important: They were trying to remember
Christ without remembering his Body, which necessarily
includes the poor and the "unacceptable." They wanted to
celebrate the Head without the Body—a risen and glorified
"sacramental" Christ separated from his actual Body *now.*

Paul's experience at his conversion had convinced him that
the risen Lord cannot be separated from his disciples; they are
one Body. He tells the Corinthians that they must examine
themselves as to which Body they are celebrating. The Christ
they are proclaiming is the risen Christ, glorified in his
members, inseparably united with the poor and marginal. This
is the Body they must see at the Eucharist if they are to
celebrate worthily, for all who eat and drink without discerning
this Body eat and drink judgment on themselves (see
1 Corinthians 11:29).

Paul reminds us of an awesome responsibility: Coming
forward during Mass to receive Holy Communion is a promise
that we will treat each person who receives the bread and drinks
the cup as a member of our own body! It is no longer "us and
them" but just "us." Sharing the meal is a promise that we will
treat all men and women as Christ would treat them—indeed,
as we would treat Christ himself. This is what it means to "do
this in memory of me"—to see in this celebration the mystery
of the risen Lord, the mystery of the interconnectedness of all
creation.

This is an enormous responsibility, one I do not think about
often enough and one that has greatly influenced my
understanding of the Eucharist. It is easy to lose sight of this
relationship: risen Christ/Mystical Body/eucharistic presence.

Catholics have always believed in the real presence of Christ in the Eucharist. We steadfastly believe that the bread is really Christ's Body, as he said, because we steadfastly believe that we who eat the bread are really Christ's Body. As the early Christians sang at Eucharist: "As many grapes are brought together and crushed to make the wine, and as many grains of wheat are ground into flour to make the one bread, so we, although many, become one Body when we eat the one Bread."[1]

Whenever I try to explain the meaning of the Eucharist, I try to focus on this relation between the Eucharist and the Easter experience of the risen Lord. In this I am following the example of Saint Paul, who reminded the Corinthians that they must discern the Body of the Lord when they celebrate the Lord's supper. I am following the example of Saint Augustine, who reminded his fourth-century parish of this same reality. He taught that the Eucharist was a "sacrament of love, a sign of unity, a bond of charity," and told them: "If, then, you are the body of Christ and his members, it is your sacrament that reposes on the altar of the Lord. Be what you see and receive what you are" (Sermon 272). "There you are on the table, and there you are in the chalice" (Sermon 229).

Achieving a Balance

Balancing the images of Good Friday, Holy Thursday and Easter Sunday (sacrifice, banquet, unity of creation) is not an easy task. Sometimes I feel like a juggler at the circus trying to keep three objects in the air at once. I am no good at juggling three objects; the best I can do is to let one drop to the floor and just hold on tightly to the other two. But when it comes to keeping these three ideas in balance, I think the Church is asking us to hold on to all three.

The opening paragraph of the Second Vatican Council's treatment of Eucharist very carefully balances these three images:

At the Last Supper [Holy Thursday], on the night when

56

he was betrayed, our Savior instituted the eucharistic sacrifice of his body and blood. He did this in order to perpetuate the sacrifice of the cross [Good Friday] throughout the centuries until he should come again and in this way to entrust to his beloved Bride, the Church, a memorial of his death and resurrection [Easter Sunday] (*Constitution on the Liturgy*, #42).

What Do Catholics Believe?

The best way to answer the question "What do Catholics believe?" is to look carefully at the prayers Catholics pray at the Eucharist. Although the words are a little different in each of the Eucharistic Prayers, the central idea is the same. At each Eucharist, we call upon our loving God and remember the great works of creation and salvation. We remember the life-giving acts of Jesus: We remember what he did with bread and wine on the night before he suffered. We petition God to "let your Spirit come upon these gifts to make them holy, so that they may become for us the body and blood of our Lord, Jesus Christ" so that "all who share in the body and blood of Christ [may] be brought together in unity by the Holy Spirit" (Eucharistic Prayer II).

At every Eucharist, we ask God to send the Spirit to do two things: (1) to transform the bread and wine so that (2) we who eat the one bread and drink the cup may become one Body. These two petitions go together: the transformation of the *elements* and the transformation of the *communicants*.

Look upon this sacrifice which you have given to your Church;
and by your Holy Spirit, gather all who share this bread and wine,
into the one body of Christ, a living sacrifice of praise.
(Eucharistic Prayer IV)

Grant that we, who are nourished by his body and blood,

may be filled with his Holy Spirit,
and become one body, one spirit in Christ.
(Eucharistic Prayer III)

When I was a child it seemed as though the emphasis was
placed on the first transformation. To be a Catholic I had to
believe that the bread and wine became the Body and Blood of
Christ. There were many ways to explain how this happened.
Transubstantiation was one explanation (based on medieval
physics and scholastic philosophy) of how this change took
place.

Today, the second transformation, the transformation of the
communicants into the Body, is the more difficult for
contemporary American Catholics. Our American culture
places a high value on the individual, on independence and
freedom from obligations to one another. I hear people saying
"I have to own a gun because no one is going to protect me but
me. The police can't even protect themselves." "I work hard for
my money. I am not going to let the government take my
money and waste it on welfare." If a culture is infected with
racism or sexism, the Christians who are formed by that culture
will find it difficult to express their devotion at a Eucharist
which proclaims that "there is no longer Jew or Greek, there is
no longer slave or free, there is no longer male and female"
(Galatians 3:28).

In Chapter Two we explored how, in our baptismal
promises, we renounced Satan by whatever names evil bears
today: racism, sexism and exaggerated individualism. As
Catholics come to the church for Eucharist, they dip their hand
in the baptismal water and renew their baptismal vows, making
the sign of the cross.

Each time we approach the Eucharist we renew that
baptismal promise. Each time we get up and go to Holy
Communion we give sign to the community that we are
committed to all that the Eucharist stands for—that we are
committed to "do this" in memory of Jesus, to live as he lived,
to live no longer for ourselves but for his Body so that the
world can say of us today as they said of the first Christians,
"See how they love one another! There is no one poor among

them!" This is the ultimate meaning of the Eucharist.

FOR PRAYER

Jesus, on the night before you died for us
  you sat at table with your friends.
In feeding them you promised
  that we would never be alone,
  that we would never be
  without your healing and saving presence.
Help me to experience your healing presence
  at each Eucharist.
May I experience the unity and the peace
  that are the signs of that Kingdom
  where you live and reign forever and ever.
Take far from me all that keeps me
  from entering into full communion with your disciples.
Free me especially from _____.
Feed me and nourish me so that I may _____.

FOR REFLECTION AND DISCUSSION

1) What is your favorite Sunday activity?

2) What is the difference between what Catholics do in church
   on Sunday and what Protestants do?

3) What does Saint Paul mean when he says "and it is no
   longer I who live, but it is Christ who lives in me"
   (Galatians 2:20a)? How is this caused by the Eucharist?

FOR FURTHER INFORMATION

Leo Hay, *Eucharist: A Thanksgiving Celebration*. Collegeville,
  Minn.: The Liturgical Press, a Michael Glazier book, 1989.

Bernard Lee, editor, *Alternative Futures for Worship: Volume*

3, *The Eucharist.* Collegeville, Minn.: The Liturgical Press, 1987.

Kenan Osborne, *The Christian Sacraments of Initiation: Baptism, Confirmation, Eucharist.* New York: Paulist Press, 1987.

Catechism of the Catholic Church, "The Sacrament of the Eucharist" (#1322-1419).

Notes

[1] Adapted from the *Didache*, an early second-century manuscript on Church doctrine and discipline (Chapter 9).

CHAPTER FIVE

A Walk Through the Mass:
What Does It Look Like?

In the previous chapter we considered the meaning of the Eucharist and saw how this meaning is expressed through the three images of Holy Thursday, Good Friday and Easter Sunday. Before moving on to consider the remaining sacraments, we will take a closer look at how the Eucharist is actually celebrated. In the last chapter we considered what it means; in this chapter we will consider what it looks like and take a brief walk through a typical Sunday Mass.

While the shape of a wedding ring is a ring—a round band of metal worn on the finger—a wedding ring means much more than just another ring. While the shape of the Mass can be described as a meal, no Catholic would say it is "just another meal." But this meal "shape" can help us map our walk through the Mass. When friends gather for a meal they sit and talk; eventually they move to the table, say grace, pass the food and eat and drink. Finally they take their leave and go home. On our walk through the Mass we will follow a similar outline: (1) gathering, (2) storytelling, (3) meal sharing and (4) commissioning.

Part One: Gathering Rites

Coming together is at the very heart of our Sunday worship. The reason behind each ritual action of the first part of the Mass can be found in this word: *gathering*. The purpose of these rites is to bring us together into one Body, ready to listen and to break bread together.

Welcome. In many churches today people will be at the door to greet you as you arrive for Sunday Mass. We all like to be greeted and welcomed when we gather for a celebration. If the greeters recognize that you are new to the parish, they will give you a special hello and be sure that you have the service books (or missalette or hymnal) necessary to pray with the assembly.

Using water. One of the first things Catholics do when they come to church is dip their right hand in water and make the Sign of the Cross. This ritual is a reminder of our Baptism: We were baptized with water and signed with the cross. At every Mass we renew and sustain the promises of our Baptism. It is Baptism that brings us to church.

Genuflection. In medieval Europe, it was a custom to go down on one knee (to genuflect) before a king or person of rank. This secular mark of honor gradually entered Church practices and people began to genuflect to honor the altar and the presence of Christ in the tabernacle. The custom of genuflecting before entering the pew was always a part of my experience of going to church when I was growing up. Today many Catholics express their reverence with an even older custom: They bow to the altar before taking their place.

Posture, song. When the Mass begins everyone stands up. Standing is the traditional posture of the Christian at prayer: It expresses our attentiveness to the word of God and our readiness to carry it out. Often we begin by singing together. What better way to gather than to unite our thoughts and our voices in common melody and words!

Greeting. The priest asks us to begin with the Sign of the Cross, again reminding us of Baptism, and will greet us with "The Lord be with you." This is a greeting you are going to hear frequently. It means many things. Like *Good day*, it can mean both "hello" and "good-bye." It is both a wish (*May* the Lord be with you) and a profound statement of faith (As you assemble for worship, the Lord *is* with you). It is an ancient biblical greeting: Boaz, returning from Bethlehem, said to the reapers, "The Lord be with you!" (Ruth 2:4). The ritual response to this greeting is always the formula, "And also with you," by which we return the hello, the good wishes, the statement of faith.

Penitential Rite, Gloria. All the ritual acts of this first part of the Mass are intended to gather us together into a worshiping assembly. We are asked to pause and recall our common need for salvation (the Penitential Rite). Sometimes the hymn "Glory to God in the Highest" is sung or recited. The *Gloria* has been a part of the Mass since about the sixth century. The words to these longer hymns and responses are found in the service book (or the missalette) at your seat.

Opening Prayer. At the close of these gathering rites the priest will ask us to join our minds in prayer. After a few moments of silence he will collect our intentions into one prayer, which we all make our own by responding "Amen."

Part Two: Storytelling

When we gather at home for a meal, we always begin with conversation—telling our stories. At Mass, after the rites of gathering, we sit down and enter into ritual conversation with the word of God—the Liturgy of the Word.

Three readings and a psalm. On Sundays there are three readings from the Bible. The first reading is from the Hebrew Scriptures. We recall the origins of our covenant. This reading will relate to the Gospel selection and will give background and insight into the meaning of the Gospel. After the reading we will sing or recite a psalm, a song from God's own inspired hymnal, the biblical Book of Psalms. The second reading is usually from one of the letters of Paul or another apostolic writing. The third reading will be taken from one of the four Gospels. The first readings conclude with the formula, "The word of the Lord" to which we all respond with our liturgical *yes*: "Thanks be to God."

Some visitors to the Catholic Mass are surprised to find Catholics reading from the Bible. We Catholics have not been generally famous for our Bible reading, and yet the Mass and the other sacraments have always been basically and fundamentally biblical. Even Catholics might be surprised to learn how much of the Mass is taken from the Bible: not only the three readings and the psalm, not only the obviously biblical prayers such as the Holy, Holy, Holy and the Lord's

Prayer, but *most* of the words and phrases of the prayers of the Mass are taken from the Bible either directly or indirectly (by using the Bible as the source of their vocabulary and imagery).

Standing for the Gospel. Because of the unique reverence given to the words of Jesus, it has long been the custom to stand in attentive reverence to hear proclamation of the Gospel. We believe that Christ "is present in his word, since it is he himself who speaks when the holy Scriptures are read in the church" (*Constitution on the Liturgy,* #7).

The priest again greets us with "The Lord be with you," and we again use our ritual response. The priest introduces the Gospel reading while making a small cross on his forehead, lips and heart with his thumb and praying silently that God will cleanse his mind and his heart so that his lips may proclaim the Gospel worthily. The congregation often performs this ritual action along with the priest. The Gospel reading concludes with the formula, "The gospel of the Lord," and we respond, "Praise to you, Lord Jesus Christ," again proclaiming our faith in the presence of Christ in the word. Then we sit for the homily.

Homily. For many years Catholics were accustomed to hearing a "sermon" at this point, a talk about how one is to live and what one is to believe without reference to the Scripture readings. *Homily* is a new word for Catholics. A homily is an act of worship rooted in the texts of the Mass and especially in the Scripture readings that have just been proclaimed. The homily takes the word of God and brings it to our life situation today. Just as a large piece of bread must be broken to feed individual persons, the word of God must be broken open to be received and digested by the congregation.

Creed. The homily is often followed by a few moments of silence, during which we each thank God for the word we have heard and during which we can apply the message of today's readings to our daily living. We then stand and together recite the creed (which can be found in the service book or missalette). The creed is a list of things we believe. Yet it is more than a list: It is a statement of our faith in the word we have heard proclaimed in the Scripture and the homily, a profession of the faith that leads us to give our lives for one another as Christ gave his life for us.

64

The creed was originally the profession of faith of those about to be baptized at this point in the Mass. Today the creed serves as a reminder of our Baptism. As we turn from the Liturgy of the Word to the Liturgy of the Eucharist, we are reminded that each time we come to the Eucharist we come through Baptism.

General Intercessions. The Liturgy of the Word (our "storytelling" part of the Mass) comes to a close with the General Intercessions.

Before you leave your home to go out to eat, you may take a look in a mirror to see if you actually look the way you want to look: hair in place, coat buttoned correctly. Perhaps you make a few last-minute adjustments so that the image in the mirror reflects your mind's image of yourself.

The General Intercessions serve a similar purpose at Mass. We are the Body of Christ by Baptism. Now, as we prepare to approach the table for Eucharist, we look into the readings, like a mirror, and ask: Is that who we are? Does the Body of Christ present in this assembly resemble that Body of Christ pictured in the Scripture readings? Usually not! And so we make some adjustments; we pray that our assembly come really to look like the Body of Christ: a body at peace, with shelter for the homeless, healing for the sick and food for the hungry. We pray that our Church and the world may come to look like the dream God has for us, the dream we have heard promised in God's word.

The petitions usually fall into four categories: We pray for the Church, for the nations and their leaders, for people in special need and for the local needs of the parish. A minister announces the petitions; we all pray for that intention in our heart; then we make some common response aloud—"Lord, hear our prayer," or another phrase that expresses our prayer.

Part Three: Meal Sharing

After the readings, we move to the table. As at a meal in the home of a friend, we (1) bring the food to the table, (2) say grace and (3) share the food. At Mass these ritual actions are

called (1) the Preparation of the Gifts, (2) the Eucharistic
Prayer, (3) the Communion Rite.

The Preparation of the Gifts

The early Christians brought some bread and wine from their
homes to the church to be used for the Mass and to be given to
the church ministers and the poor. Today a similar offering for
the parish and the poor is made with our monetary
contributions. Members of the parish take up a collection from
the assembly and bring it to the priest along with the bread and
wine that will be used for the sacrifice.

The priest ritually places the bread and wine on the table.
He mixes water with the wine and washes his hands to help us
think of the Last Supper. (Mixing water with wine and washing
hands are things all Jews did at meals in Jesus' day.) The priest
then invites us to pray that the sacrifice be acceptable to God.
We respond "Amen" to the Prayer Over the Gifts and stand to
begin the central prayer of the Mass.

The Eucharistic Prayer

The long prayer that follows brings us to the very center of the
Mass and the heart of our Catholic faith. While the words of the
prayer may vary from Sunday to Sunday, the prayer always has
this structure: (1) We remember all God's wonderful saving
deeds. (2) We recall the central event in our history, Jesus
Christ, and in particular the memorial he left us on the night
before he died. We recall his passion, death and resurrection.
(3) As we gratefully remember all the wonderful things God
has done for us in the past, we petition God to continue those
deeds of Christ in the present and future: We pray that we may
become one Body, one Spirit in Christ.

Invitation. The prayer begins with a dialogue between the
leader and the assembly. First, the greeting we discussed
above: "The Lord be with you." The priest then asks if we are
ready and willing to approach the table and to renew our
baptismal commitment, offering ourselves to God: "Lift up
your hearts." And we say that we are prepared to do so: "We lift
them up to the Lord." The priest invites us to give thanks to the
Lord our God. And we respond: "It is right to give him thanks

and praise." "Thanks and praise" translates the traditional Greek verb which names the whole action: *Eucharist.*

Preface and Acclamation. The priest enters into the Preface. This is not a preface in the sense of an introduction that is not really a part of the story, but a preface in the Latin meaning of the word, "before the face"—a coming before the face of God. Brought into God's presence, we speak of how wonderful God has been to us. As the wonders of God are told, the assembly cannot hold back their joy. They sing aloud, in effect: "Wow! Wow! Wow! What a wonderful God we have!" In the ritual language of the Mass, this acclamation takes the form: "Holy, holy, holy Lord, God of power and might,/heaven and earth are full of your glory."

The narrative of the institution. The priest continues the prayer, giving praise and thanks, and calls upon the Holy Spirit to change our gifts of bread and wine into the Body and Blood of Christ. The priest then recalls the events of the Last Supper and tells the narrative or story of the institution of the Eucharist. We are then invited to "proclaim the mystery of faith." Several texts are possible, for example: "Christ has died, Christ has risen, Christ will come again." The priest continues recalling the wonderful deeds of salvation: the passion, death and resurrection of Christ.

Prayer for Unity and Intercessions. The grateful memory of God's salvation leads us to make a bold petition—our main petition at every Eucharist. We pray for unity: "May all of us who share in the body and blood of Christ be brought together in unity by the Holy Spirit" (Eucharistic Prayer II).

To this petition for unity we add prayers for the bishop of Rome and for the bishop of the local Church; we pray for the living and the dead and especially for ourselves, that through the intercession of the saints we may one day arrive at the table in heaven, of which this table is only a hint and a taste.

We look forward to that glorious day and raise our voices with those of all the saints before us as the priest raises the bread and wine and offers a toast, a doxology or prayer of glory to God in the name of Christ: "Through him, with him, and in him, in the unity of the Holy Spirit,/all glory and honor is yours, almighty Father, for ever and ever." Our "Amen" to this prayer acclaims our assent and participation in the entire Eucharistic Prayer.

The Communion Rite

Our Father and Sign of Peace. We prepare to eat and drink at the Lord's table with the words taught us by Jesus: "Give us this day our daily bread; and forgive us our trespasses as we forgive those who trespass against us." Communion (the word means "union with") is the sign and source of our reconciliation and union with God and with one another. Therefore, we make a gesture of union and forgiveness with those around us: We offer them a Sign of Peace.

Invitation to Communion. The priest then shows us the bread and wine and invites us to come to the table: "This is the Lamb of God..../Happy are those who are called to his supper." The members of the assembly approach the altar in procession.

Communion. As God fed our ancestors in the desert on their pilgrimage, so God gives us food for our journey. We approach the minister, who gives us the eucharistic bread with the words, "The body of Christ." We respond "Amen." We then go to the minister with the cup who gives it to us with the words, "The blood of Christ," to which we again profess our "Amen." During this procession we usually sing a hymn which unites our voices, minds and thoughts even as the Body and Blood of Christ unites our bodies. Then we pray silently in our hearts, asking for all that this sacrament promises. The priest unites our prayers in the *Prayer After Communion*, to which we respond "Amen."

Part Four: Commissioning

Announcements. Finally we prepare to go back to that world in which we will live for the coming week. The burdens we have laid down at the door of the church for this Eucharist we know we must bear again—but now, we bear them strengthened by this Eucharist and this community. Announcements at this time remind us of important activities of the parish during the coming week. The priest again says, "The Lord be with you."

This ritual phrase serves now as a farewell.

Blessing and Dismissal. We bow our heads to receive a blessing. As the priest names the Trinity, we make the Sign of the Cross as at the beginning of the Mass. The priest or deacon then dismisses the assembly: "Go in peace...." And we give our liturgical yes, "Thanks be to God."

In Latin this dismissal is *Ite, missa est.* The word *missa* is probably the origin of the name most American Catholics use for the Eucharist, Mass.

We leave the assembly and the church building, but we carry something with us. For example, a newly married couple leave their wedding ceremony but carry their marriage with them. What happens in the days and years after the wedding gives deeper meaning to the symbols they have exchanged (their wedding rings, for example). And what happens in our lives during the week gives deeper meaning to the ritual actions we have celebrated at Mass. As we daily carry our brokenness for love of the Crucified, we find ever deeper meaning in the broken bread. As we pour out our lives in love for the homeless, the alienated, Christ's little ones, we find meaning in the cup poured out. It is only in relation to our daily lives that the full meaning of the ritual actions of the Mass become clear.

I have seen the simplest of wedding rings worn with pride and fidelity by couples in poverty working to grow in their love for one another. I have seen loveless marriages symbolized in rings with diamonds the size of blueberries, but the ring was "just another piece of jewelry"; all meaning had gone out of it. It is not the splendor of the ring but the meaning which gives it value.

I have celebrated Mass with popes and with prisoners. I have seen the Mass celebrated in grand cathedrals and humble rural churches. And I have come to realize that it is not the splendor of the ceremonies but the faith of the participants that will most eloquently tell you what the Mass is. I have experienced Mass in the simplest of settings with Catholics whose faith and love were so evident that even a visitor could sense that, like the disciples of Emmaus, these Christians truly "recognized him in the breaking of the bread" (see Luke 24:13-35).

FOR PRAYER

Loving Jesus, at the Eucharist I experience
  your continuing presence and protection.
At each Mass may I join more closely
  with those whom you love.
May I hear your word
  and bring it into my heart
  that it may re-form my life.
I want to proclaim your death
  by my own life poured out.
May I take up my cross each day as I _____.

May this sacred meal strengthen me
  so that I may be able to _____.
May my life be filled with Eucharist,
  filled with thanks and praise
  for all the blessings you have given me,
  especially for _____.

FOR REFLECTION AND DISCUSSION

1) Why do we read from the Bible each time we assemble for
Eucharist?

2) What does it mean to say that the Mass is a meal? What does
it mean to say that the Mass is a sacrifice?

3) How does the shape of the Mass differ from the shape of
Sunday services in other Christian Churches?

FOR FURTHER INFORMATION

Robert Cabié, *History of the Mass*. Washington, D.C.: Pastoral
Press, 1992.

Regis Duffy, *Real Presence: Worship, Sacraments, and
Commitment*. San Francisco: Harper and Row, 1982.

Tad Guzie, *Jesus and the Eucharist*. Ramsey, N.J.: Paulist

Press, 1974.

Lawrence Johnson, *The Mystery of Faith: A Study of the Structural Elements of the Order of Mass*. Washington, D.C.: Federation of Diocesan Liturgical Commissions, 1982.

William Marrevee, *The Popular Guide to the Mass*. Washington, D.C.: Pastoral Press, 1992.

Catechism of the Catholic Church, "The Sacrament of the Eucharist" (#1345-1355).

CHAPTER SIX

Celebrating What Jesus Does:
Reconciliation

We have journeyed through the basic sacraments, those common to all Christians. The next sacraments we will discuss, the sacraments of healing and vocation, are of a different sort: They are not for everyone, nor do they have the same biblical mandate as do the sacraments of initiation. We will first discuss the Sacrament of Reconciliation (or "confession," as it is sometimes called).

"Why do I have to tell my sins to a priest?" "How can a priest forgive sins? I thought only God could forgive sins." "Confession? I didn't think Catholics did that anymore." I hear these questions and statements frequently, and they are but one indication that the Sacrament of Reconciliation is often misunderstood by Catholics and non-Catholics alike. The way Catholics celebrate the Sacrament of Reconciliation today can only be understood by looking at history. And for that reason our tour will pass through the history of this sacrament in some detail.

Jesus: Sacrament of Reconciliation

Before we begin to examine the complicated history of Reconciliation, it is good to recall that it all starts with Jesus. Jesus is the basic reconciling sacrament. The entire life of Jesus, his entire mission, can be viewed as a ministry of reconciliation. The mysterious plan of God as revealed in the Scriptures is a vision of unity and harmony. Jesus came to make visible this desire of the invisible God to reconcile all creation and to bring it to wholeness and unity.

We know from our own lived experience how far we are

from the actual achievement of God's dreams for the world. The world is scarred by sin. Yet the life of Jesus reveals God's loving hand mercifully stretched out to sinners, and his life culminates as he opens his arms on the cross, embracing all sinners. By his death he put an end to death.

Forgiveness of Sin in the Early Church

The Church continues Jesus' ministry of reconciliation. This is accomplished primarily in the sacraments of Christian initiation. All sins are forgiven when a person is plunged into the death and resurrection of Jesus. Baptism changes everything! The time of sinning is over! As Saint Paul says:

> So if anyone is in Christ, there is a new creation: everything old has passed away; see, everything has become new! All this is from God, who reconciled us to himself through Christ, and has given us the ministry of reconciliation; that is, in Christ God was reconciling the world to himself, not counting their trespasses against them, and entrusting the message of reconciliation to us. So we are ambassadors for Christ, since God is making his appeal through us; we entreat you on behalf of Christ, be reconciled to God. For our sake he made him to be sin who knew no sin, so that in him we might become the righteousness of God.
> (2 Corinthians 5:17-21)

For the early Church, the Sunday celebration of the Eucharist was the weekly renewal of baptismal promises. In the Eucharist the baptized received that bread which was given for the forgiveness of sins. The sins committed after Baptism were forgiven by prayer, almsgiving, fasting, self-denial and especially by the Eucharist. For many centuries the Eucharist was the primary and only sacrament of reconciliation.

Canonical Penance: Second Baptism

Despite the long and rigorous conversion process preceding the sacraments of initiation, there were times when some members of the community fell into grave, public, scandalous sin after Baptism. During the time of the Roman persecutions, in particular, some of the baptized denied that they were Christians and reneged on their baptismal promises. In these cases the community felt it could not in conscience join around the eucharistic table and break bread with such persons. The unity with Christ and with the Church which the Eucharist proclaimed was not authentic until such persons repented and did penance for their crimes.

The Church developed a ritual for this reconciliation process. The model that the community had at hand was the ritual of Baptism. While the community knew that no one should enter the baptismal bath a second time, a rite developed that was modeled on the catechumenate. This rite, which we have come to call "canonical penance" because it was legislated by the *canons* or *laws* of the Church, consisted of several steps. The sinner came to the leader of the community (the bishop) and they talked privately. The sinner then came before the community at the Sunday eucharistic assembly. There, in the presence of the whole assembly, the sinner entered the "Order of Penitents." This rite was similar to that which we might see today when we see people entering the Order of Catechumens. The leader of the community prayed for the penitent and imposed hands in a gesture of blessing and healing. A penance was assigned and the penitent was invested in a special garment. The time of penance was long—lasting several years or even the rest of the person's life.

You could only become a penitent once. Just as Baptism was a once-in-a-lifetime event, so was canonical penance, the second Baptism. During the time of penance the penitent would come to church as the assembly gathered for Eucharist and would stand or kneel at the door and ask for the prayers of the community. The community was deeply involved in every step of the conversion process. Just as the community was wounded by the sin, so the community aided in the reconciliation:

praying, guiding, giving example, sponsoring.

After several years, the penitent was permitted to enter the assembly to hear the word of God and the homily. These Scripture readings and instructions were an integral part of the conversion process.

Finally, the great day came when the period of penance was over. At Mass, after the readings and the homily, the penitent approached the bishop. They exchanged a kiss of peace and the penitent was embraced back into the community. The penitent entered into Communion with them by sharing in the breaking of the bread. This often took place on Holy Thursday so that the penitent would be able to enter fully into the sacred liturgies of the Triduum: Good Friday, Holy Saturday and Easter.

Tariff Penance: A Doctor Visit

In the fifth century, on the islands we now call Ireland and England, a different type of penance came to be practiced. In the monasteries of that time arose the custom of going to a holy person to ask for help and advice to overcome sin. Just as a person today would go to a doctor to ask for help and advice in overcoming a physical illness, so the Christian in fifth-century Ireland would seek out a holy person (often a monk) to find a remedy for a spiritual illness. The spiritual medicine of the day consisted of "healing by opposites." Gluttony could be healed by fasting, laziness by rising early for prayer. This is the origin of what historians now call "tariff penance."

This tariff system ("tariff" here means a list or scale of prices or charges) was very different from the canonical penance practiced on the continent. Canonical penance was for grave public sins; this tariff penance was for all sins. Canonical penance was possible only once; tariff penance was repeatable (just as visiting a doctor is repeatable). Note also that canonical penance involved the whole parish community and was accompanied by liturgical rites; the Celtic tariff penance was a private affair. To understand canonical penance think "Baptism"; to understand tariff penance think "doctor visit."

Confession: Coming Before the Judge

The Irish missionaries brought tariff penance to the continent. It met initially with official resistance on the part of the bishops, but soon private penance became the common practice in the Church. For some years it existed side by side with canonical penance, but eventually it evolved into sacramental confession.

The evolution from tariff penance to confession is difficult to trace in detail. Several important changes in the sacrament took place: The confession itself, the telling of the sins, became so important that the whole rite began to be called "confession." The confession was not primarily to a holy man who knew good remedies for sin, but to a priest who had the *power* to give absolution. The penance the sinner was to perform was greatly reduced—six Our Fathers in place of fasting on bread and water. In both canonical and tariff systems the penance was accomplished *before* the reconciliation with the community; in confession, the penance was done *after* absolution.

The model shifted from Baptism or doctor visit to a judicial trial, a coming before the judge. The Church began to be concerned with issues of jurisdiction (the judge must be competent in the case) and telling the sins accurately (the judge must have accurate knowledge on which to base his decision). The principal focus was on the judgment itself, the juridical pronouncement of absolution. This judicial model of the sacrament was the one I learned as a child and the one which I practiced during the first years of my priestly ministry.

Confessions of Devotion

In the course of time, Christians who were not excommunicated or who had not committed serious public crimes also began to enter "into penance." Good Christians began to come forward on Ash Wednesday along with the formal penitents and ask for ashes and a formal penance so that they too might atone for their sins during Lent. The sacramental rituals for the public reconciliation of grave sinners were appropriated by good and pious Christians as an ascetical practice to help them grow in the spiritual life. During the early days of my priesthood long lines of such good and pious Catholics came to confession each Saturday afternoon.

In the years immediately preceding the Second Vatican Council, something happened to all this. Perhaps we are still too close to the event to know exactly what it was that caused the change. But the long lines for confession on Saturday afternoon little by little disappeared.

I personally do not believe that this change came about because Catholics stopped sinning. Nor do I believe that Catholics suddenly lost a sense of sin or no longer felt the need for forgiveness and reconciliation. But in any case things were changing; and in a time of transition and change, it is important to know which things are truly important and which things are secondary.

What's Most Important

What is the most important thing about the Sacrament of Reconciliation? I learned the answer to this question from a saintly and learned German pastor, Father Bernard Häring, long before the Second Vatican Council revised the way Catholics go to confession. One summer I was taking a course from Father Häring and he told a story which prepared me for the changes to come by radically altering the way in which I think about this sacrament:

> One Sunday afternoon in the 1930's in a little parish in Germany where he was pastor, Father Häring was leading the customary Sunday afternoon parish Vespers service with religious instruction and Benediction. This particular Sunday he was talking about confession.
>
> He began by asking the congregation: "What is the most important thing about confession?" A woman in the front pew immediately responded: "Telling your

78

sins to the priest. That's why we call it *confession*."
Father Häring said, "Confessing the sins is important,
but it's not the most important thing."

A man toward the back called out: "Contrition!
Being sorry for your sins! The whole thing doesn't
work without contrition." Father Häring said, "It
doesn't 'work' without contrition, but I don't think
that contrition is the most important thing."

A man over on one side of the church spoke up:
"It's the examination of conscience. Unless you
examine your conscience, you don't know what you
have to be sorry for and you don't know what to
confess. Anybody can see that the examination of
conscience is the most important thing." Father Häring
wasn't satisfied with this answer either.

A young woman on the aisle tried: "It's the
penance—giving back the things you stole. Unless you
do the penance, it doesn't count."

The congregation could tell by Father Häring's
face that he still hadn't heard the most important thing.
An uneasy silence fell over the church as people tried
to think. In the silence a little girl in the third pew said:
"Father, I know what's most important. It's what Jesus
does."

It's what Jesus does! That's the most important
thing, the thing we should focus upon. The
examination of conscience, sorrow for sin, telling the
sins to the priest, acts of satisfaction—these are all
important. But the focus must be on what is most
important, *what Jesus does.*

Reconciliation Today: Think Baptism

The Second Vatican Council wanted to restore Jesus as the
focus of this sacrament. Because the Eucharist is the model
sacrament, the new Sacrament of Reconciliation resembles the
Eucharist. It is a public liturgical act where the community, the
Body of Christ, gathers to hear the word of God and to receive

79

signs of God's graced presence.

The new *Rite of Penance*, published in 1973, lists three ways of celebrating the Sacrament of Reconciliation. The second form of the sacrament, the Rite for Reconciliation of Several Penitents with Individual Confession and Absolution (a communal penance service), is the form most Catholics use today and the one that you who are reading this book are most likely to experience.

Since Eucharist is the model for all the sacraments, the outline of the Eucharist given in Chapter Four is operative here also. The ritual gives many choices to the local community, so it is impossible to say *exactly* what a communal celebration of the Sacrament of Reconciliation will look like. It will, however, look something like this:

Gathering Rites. As the community gathers, ministers of hospitality at the door of the church say hello and give us a service program listing the hymns, the prayers we will say aloud and any directions we may need to participate in the service. A typical gathering rite consists of a hymn, a liturgical greeting and a prayer by the priest leading the celebration.

Storytelling. Once we are gathered, we tell the stories of God's love and mercy as recorded in the Bible. The shape of this part of the rite will probably remind you of Sunday Mass, with readings from the Hebrew and Christian Scriptures, a Gospel and a homily.

Responding to the Word of God. Having heard how much God loves us, we examine our lives to see how well we have loved God in return. After a time to examine our conscience in the light of the Scriptures we have heard, we will express our sorrow together in an Act of Contrition. This will be followed by a procession of the congregation to the priest(s) to tell our sins and to hear the proclamation of God's forgiveness.

Celebrating Reconciliation. We have responded to the Word of God; now we celebrate God's response to our word. This part of the celebration typically includes a hymn, a proclamation of praise and thanksgiving for God's mercy, the Lord's Prayer, a Sign of Peace, a song of thanksgiving and a concluding prayer.

Commissioning. The rite concludes with prayers, blessings

80

and dismissal. Often the sacrament is followed by a parish reception, depending upon the occasion and the liturgical season.

What Happened to Confession?

Names are important. The Sacrament of Reconciliation has been called different things. In the recent past, bishops, theologians and Church documents have consistently called this sacrament the "Sacrament of Penance" and called those going to the sacrament "penitents." This language has never been popular with ordinary Catholics, who used the names *confession, confessor* and *confessional. Confession,* however, only names one part of the sacrament and not the most important part at that. *Reconciliation* names what is most important, what Jesus does. "Sacrament of Reconciliation" is the name used in the rite itself and was the name preferred by Pope Paul VI, who issued the new rite.

The transition from private confession to a communal, public celebration of the sacrament is not merely a change of ceremonies. It has come about primarily because of a change in the way in which we understand sin. When I was growing up, it seemed that nothing was more personal and private than my sins. Now I find that this is only partly true: Our sins are personal, but they are never private. Pope John Paul II clearly affirmed that "there is no sin, not even the most intimate and secret one, the most strictly individual one, that exclusively concerns the person committing it. With greater or lesser violence, with greater or lesser harm, every sin has repercussions on the entire ecclesial body and the whole human family."[1]

As sin affects the community, so Reconciliation affects the community—and a communal celebration of the sacrament says this most eloquently. The general norms for the liturgical reform given by the Second Vatican Council state that "whenever rites, according to their specific nature, make provision for communal celebration involving the presence and active participation of the faithful, it is to be stressed that this

81

way of celebrating them is to be preferred, as far as possible, to a celebration that is individual and, so to speak, private" (*Constitution on the Liturgy*, #27). The new *Rite* itself states that "communal celebration shows more clearly the ecclesial nature of penance" (#22). Pope Paul VI, after promulgating the revised rite, told a general audience on April 3, 1974, that he hoped the communal rite would "become the normal way of celebration." And indeed this is the rite which has become popular in Catholic parishes.

Why do Catholics go to a priest? There are many reasons why you might want to talk to a priest: You may want advice, counseling, moral guidance, help with your marriage, spiritual direction. Or you may be lonely and just want to talk to someone. It is important to note that none of these reasons require a *priest*. Indeed, a priest may not even be the best person to meet these needs for you.

More importantly, none of these things is the principal focus of the Sacrament of Reconciliation. The sacrament is the proclamation of reconciliation with God and with the Church. The other reasons for talking to a priest mentioned above are separate and distinct things. They each have their own way of working best. And they work best *outside* the sacrament.

Catholics find that the Sacrament of Reconciliation works best when they have already achieved some degree of reconciliation *before* celebrating the sacrament. Confessing "I am an alcoholic" is no substitute for going to A.A. Confessing that "my wife [husband] and I have started to yell and hit one another" is no substitute for seeking marriage counseling. Telling a confessor, "I get so angry when the neighbor's children play outside my bedroom window when I am trying to sleep" is no substitute for speaking to the neighbor directly.

Sin, in Christian perspective, is not merely breaking the rules. As we grow and mature, our internal list of rules (what some call the superego) grows also; we gather more and more *shoulds* and *oughts*. Whenever we break one of these rules, intentionally or not, we feel guilty.

Guilt is not the same as sin. For the mature Christian, sin is understood in relation to love. God has loved us so much, and we have so often failed to return that love. When we examine

82

our lives in the light of the message of Jesus, we find that Jesus calls us to wholeness, to maturity. He came that we "may have life, and have it abundantly" (see John 10:10). For an adult Christian, sin is more than just breaking the rules; sin is the failure to grow. Sin is being today like you were yesterday. Sin is the failure to respond to the love God has shown us in Christ Jesus. This is why the proclamation of the word of God has such a prominent place in the Sacrament of Reconciliation. It is the word of God which convicts us of sin and which invites us to conversion.

The Gift of Peace and Wholeness

"Peace be with you. As the Father has sent me, so I send you" (John 20:21b). Peace is the Easter gift of the risen Lord. Christ commissioned his followers to continue his mission of healing, forgiveness and reconciliation, his mission of bringing peace. Peace is the "gift" of the Sacrament of Reconciliation. Our word of sorrow meets God's word of forgiveness and explodes into *shalom*: wholeness, peace. This is why we can speak of *celebrating* the Sacrament of Reconciliation. We celebrate the gift of peace.

People tell me that they worry about "what other parishioners will think if they see me go to the priest" or "what the priest will think if I tell him...." It will probably not come as any surprise to your family and friends that you have sins to confess. (If you can't think of any, they can probably name a few!) Everybody sins. The beautiful thing is that some sinners are moved to repentance; some are willing to change. Our getting up, going to a priest and hearing the absolution is a sign to all who see us that we are one of those who wishes to repent, to do better, to live more fully the promises of our Baptism. People fear that the priest sees them at their worst. Actually it's the very opposite: The priest sees you at your best. The priest sees you not in your sinning but in your repentance.

When I was first ordained I worried about when I could give absolution and when I had to refuse it. Slowly I began to realize that the real problem is not in *giving* absolution but in helping people to *hear* it! Too few people actually hear and experience, "Go in peace, your sins are forgiven." But those who do hear know they have received a gift. Why do I celebrate Reconciliation? Why do I go to confession? Because I receive it: *shalom*, peace, wholeness.

FOR PRAYER

> Merciful God,
>> your Son, Jesus, opened his arms on the cross
>> and embraced sinners into your overwhelming
>>> forgiveness.
>
> Forgive me my sins
>> as I forgive those who sin against me.
>
> Especially help me to forgive _____.
>
> Loving Jesus, you came that we might have abundant life.
>
> Save me from all that holds me back
>> from peace and wholeness and reconciliation.
>
> Free me from _____.
>
> Strengthen in me the spirit of _____.

FOR REFLECTION AND DISCUSSION

1) Do you think the Catholic Sacrament of Reconciliation has positive value or is it something that other Churches are better off without? Why?

2) Are you comfortable with the thought of telling your sins to a priest? Why or why not?

3) Are you familiar with the practice of spiritual direction? Do you have a spiritual director? (If you are a catechumen, your sponsor or godparent might well serve as spiritual director.)

FOR FURTHER INFORMATION

Committee for Pastoral Research and Practices, National

Conference of Catholic Bishops, *Reflections on the Sacrament of Penance in Catholic Life Today: A Study Document*. Washington, D.C.: Office for Publishing and Promotion Services, United States Catholic Conference, 1990.

James Dallen, *The Reconciling Community: The Rite of Penance*. New York: Pueblo Publishing Company, 1986.

Monika Hellwig, *Sign of Reconciliation and Conversion: The Sacrament of Penance for Our Times*. Collegeville, Minn.: The Liturgical Press, a Michael Glazier book, 1982.

Robert Kennedy, editor, *Reconciliation: The Continuing Agenda*. Collegeville, Minn.: The Liturgical Press, 1987.

Kenan Osborne, *Reconciliation and Justification*. New York: Paulist Press, 1990.

Thomas Richstatter, *The Reconciliation of Penitents*. Washington, D.C.: Federation of Diocesan Liturgical Commissions Publications, 1988.

Catechism of the Catholic Church, "The Sacrament of Penance and Reconciliation" (#1422-1498).

Notes

[1]Pope John Paul II, *Reconciliation and Penance*.

CHAPTER SEVEN

Healing the Sick:
Anointing

A few years ago when I was asked to write on the Anointing of
the Sick, I decided to reread the Gospels to find instances
where Jesus healed the sick. I thought that I was pretty familiar
with the Gospels, but I can still remember how surprised I was
to see how many passages recount the healing ministry of
Jesus.

For example, at the beginning of Mark's Gospel, Jesus calls
the first disciples, cures a man with an unclean spirit, and then
cures Peter's mother-in-law, who is in bed with a fever. That
same evening, "they brought him all who were sick or
possessed with demons. And the whole city was gathered
around the door" (Mark 1:32-33). Jesus cured many different
types of illnesses, even the most terrible afflictions of his day.
And as a result of these many cures, "Jesus could no longer go
into a town openly, but stayed out in the country; and people
came to him from every quarter" (Mark 1:45).

And all this in only the *first chapter* of Mark's Gospel!
Jesus' story has hardly begun and already he is known as one
who heals and cares for the sick.

Jesus gives us a sign, a sacrament of God's desire for our
health and wholeness. Jesus is the original sacrament of
healing. Jesus "spoke to them about the kingdom of God, and
healed those who needed to be healed" (Luke 9:11b). Jesus
commissioned the Twelve to continue his ministry in word and
work. "So they went out and proclaimed that all should repent.
They cast out many demons, and anointed with oil many who
were sick and cured them" (Mark 6:12-13).

87

Concern for the Sick in the Early Church

The healing ministry of Jesus is to be continued by the Church, as we see from the ending of Mark's Gospel. There the risen Christ tells the Eleven, "Go into all the world and proclaim the good news to the whole creation.... And these signs will accompany those who believe: ...they will lay their hands on the sick, and they will recover" (Mark 16:15b, 17a, 18b).

We read of the way in which one community continued the healing mission of Jesus in the Epistle of James:

> Are any among you suffering? They should pray. Are any cheerful? They should sing songs of praise. Are any among you sick? They should call for the elders of the church and have them pray over them, anointing them with oil in the name of the Lord. The prayer of faith will save the sick, and the Lord will raise them up; and anyone who has committed sins will be forgiven. Therefore confess your sins to one another, and pray for one another, so that you may be healed. The prayer of the righteous is powerful and effective. (James 5:13-16)

James tells us that prayer is *necessary in every situation* in our lives—in good spirits and in sickness and at every stage in between. Prayer is mentioned in every verse of this passage. It is in this context of prayer that James tells us of his community's practice of praying for the sick. The sick person takes the initiative and calls for the priests. When they arrive, they pray. The phrase "to pray over the sick person" suggests a laying on of hands. They anoint the sick with oil (the community was familiar with the use of oil as a healing ointment). They do this "in the name," that is, acting with the authority of the Lord. The atmosphere is one of intense mutual prayer. The community prays for the sick person and the sick person prays for the community.

Vatican II and the Sacrament of Anointing

The Second Vatican Council restored the Sacrament of the Anointing of the Sick to the same context of prayer and mutual concern that we find in the Epistle of James. The Anointing of the Sick had suffered many distortions with the passage of time. It had been given the name "Extreme Unction" (the "last anointing" or "anointing *in extremis*") and had been turned into a sacrament for the dying. Extreme Unction was feared by many; it was usually postponed until the last moments of life. Often no one was present but the dying person and the priest. This was a situation which needed to be corrected.

The Sacrament of the Anointing of the Sick as celebrated by Roman Catholics today may take several forms. It may be celebrated in a parish church during Sunday Eucharist. It may be celebrated in the home of a sick person or in the hospital or in emergency situations. As you are most likely to encounter the Anointing of the Sick during Sunday Mass, I will walk with you through that form of the sacrament. Again, the rite will have movements similar to those we discussed in Chapter Five, "A Walk Through the Mass."

The parish community gathers to express concern for those who are ill and those who have special needs. The sick and the congregation may be blessed with baptismal water as a reminder that the dying with Christ promised in Baptism is *real* dying experienced in the current suffering of those about to be anointed. In Baptism Christ, who suffered for us, transformed our suffering into victory.

Once we are gathered we read from the Scriptures—usually the readings assigned for the Sunday. Nearly every page of Scripture speaks of God's desire for our health and healing. Sometimes readings particularly appropriate to this theme may be chosen.

Following the readings, the priest will speak of the Christian meaning of suffering and how suffering has been redeemed by the suffering of Christ. Suffering is indeed a mystery and can never be explained. But in Christ we can find meaning in our suffering.

Suffering and illness have always been among the greatest problems that trouble the human spirit. Christians feel and experience pain as do all other people; yet their faith helps them to grasp more deeply the mystery of suffering and to bear their pain with greater courage. From Christ's words they know that sickness has meaning and value for their own salvation and the salvation of the world. They also know that Christ, who during his life often visited and healed the sick, loves them in their illness. (*Pastoral Care of the Sick*, #1)

After the homily the congregation joins in a litany of intercession for the sick, for the parish and for the needs of the world. Those to be anointed then come to the presiding minister. In silence he lays his hands on the head of each person.

Imposition of Hands

One of the key symbolic actions of the Sacrament of Anointing is this imposition of hands. The Gospels contain a number of instances in which Jesus healed the sick by the laying on of hands or even by the simple gesture of touch.

This gesture is rich in meaning. With it the priest indicates that this particular person is object of the Church's prayer of faith. The laying on of hands is a sign of blessing, as we pray that by the power of God's healing grace the sick person may be restored to health, or at least strengthened in time of illness. Above all, it is the biblical gesture of healing and, indeed, Jesus' own usual manner of healing. People brought their sick friends and relatives to him and "he laid hands on each of them and cured them" (see Luke 4:40).

The meaning of a symbol is tied up with our memories. Do you have pleasant memories of having been touched lovingly by another? Do you have unhappy memories of touch—of being hassled, pushed and shoved in a crowd? Do you have memories of the imposition of hands in other sacraments you have received? I cannot remember my Baptism, but I can recall Confirmation, when the bishop placed his hands on my head and called upon the Holy Spirit to heal and strengthen me. I remember the bishop imposing hands at my ordination to the priesthood. When I celebrate the Sacrament of Reconciliation, I experience the imposition of hands during the prayer of absolution. When the priest places his hands on my head during the Anointing of the Sick, how different this touch feels from so many of the other ways my body is touched and handled when I am sick: examined, explored, cut into. Even the loving and gentle touches of doctors and nurses I often find annoying or embarrassing. This sacramental touch, this imposition of hands, is different. In this touch I feel the Church continuing the healing touch of Jesus.

Blessing Over the Oil

Next, the leader will bless God for the gift of oil. The oil used is simply olive oil—just like that you would buy in the grocery store. (In place of olive oil, oil derived from other plants may be used.) What makes the oil special—sacramental—is the blessing said over it. This central prayer of the sacrament follows the same structure as the central prayer of the Mass, the Eucharistic Prayer: We invoke God; we gratefully remember all that God has done for us, and then we make our petition. At the Eucharist the petition is for unity; in this sacrament the petition is for healing.

The priest will use oil that has already been blessed by the bishop of the diocese. This shows in a special way the concern of the bishop and the whole diocese for the sick. Sometimes the oil will be blessed during the rite and the congregation will hear the words of praise and blessing:

> God of all consolation
> you chose and sent your Son to heal the world.
> Graciously listen to our prayer of faith;
> send the power of your Holy Spirit, the Consoler,
> into this precious oil, this soothing ointment,

this rich gift, this fruit of the earth.
Bless this oil and sanctify it for our use.
Make this oil a remedy for all who are anointed with it;
heal them in body, in soul, and in spirit,
and deliver them from every affliction.
We ask this through our Lord Jesus Christ, your Son,
who lives and reigns with you and the Holy Spirit,
one God, for ever and ever. Amen. (*Pastoral Care of the Sick*, #123)

What does this prayer say about God? About the oil? What does the prayer ask for the sick? Thoughtful meditation on this blessing is one of the best ways to prepare to celebrate the sacrament.

The Anointing

Following the blessing, the priest anoints the sick with the blessed oil. First, he makes the Sign of the Cross with the oil on their foreheads, saying: "Through this holy anointing may the Lord in his love and mercy help you with the grace of the Holy Spirit." All respond: "Amen." Then the priest anoints the palms of their hands with the Sign of the Cross, saying: "May the Lord who frees you from sin save you and raise you up." All respond: "Amen."

In the time of Jesus oil was the best medicine around. People would drink it (here I think of castor oil, even though I would rather not!). They would rub oil on their bodies as an ointment to heal and strengthen and preserve. For example, in the story of the Good Samaritan, when the Samaritan found the man who had fallen prey to robbers, he was moved to pity at the sight, dressed his wounds and poured oil on them (see Luke 10:34). When Jesus commissioned the Twelve and began to send them out two by two, giving them authority over unclean spirits, they "anointed with oil many who were sick and cured them" (Mark 6:13b).

And when I think of *olive* oil, I remember Jesus' own suffering and anxiety in the Garden of Olives.

Once again our memories are important for the meaning of the symbol. How do you feel towards oil? I *like* oil (with perhaps the exception of castor oil). I associate many pleasant sensations with oil: lotion on chapped hands after washing dishes; soothing ointment on a sore muscle; suntan lotion at the beach (I really like that one!); melted butter over hot popcorn (I know the doctor says no, but popcorn really tastes better with butter on it); oil and vinaigrette on fresh salad. The list could go on and on. I have good memories of oil. And very special among my memories is the memory of the time I was anointed with oil in the Sacrament of the Sick.

Following the anointing, the Eucharist continues as usual with the meal sharing and commissioning described in Chapter Five.

What Does It Mean?

In the liturgy our sanctification is brought about by signs perceptible to the senses. Signs are both given and received. In the Sacrament of the Sick a sign is given by the Church to the sick person, and the one who is sick gives a sign to the community.

The care and concern of the community is a sign to the sick person of the Lord's own great concern for the bodily and spiritual welfare of the sick. We who are the Body of Christ must continue to proclaim the Kingdom of wholeness and salvation in word and deed. We are a Church of healing and reconciliation. The celebration of the Sacrament of the Anointing of the Sick is a ritual moment which makes visible and present to the sick and to the whole community an image of who we are as Church: a community of mutual healing and support.

The sick in return offer a sign to the community: In this sacrament they give witness to their promises at Baptism to die and be buried with Christ crucified. They tell the community that they are prepared to fill up in their flesh what is lacking in Christ's sufferings for the salvation of the world (see Colossians 1:24; Romans 8:19-22).

93

This exchange of signs—this witness and communication between the sick and the healthy members of the community—is at the heart of the sacrament. The sick are assured in the ritual that their suffering is not "useless" but has meaning and value for their own salvation and the salvation of the world. At the same time, the Church asks the Lord to lighten their suffering and save them (see James 5:14-16). The community recognizes the sick as productive members, contributing to the welfare of all by associating themselves freely with Christ's passion and death. In the sacrament, the sick embody for us the words addressed to Timothy:

> The saying is sure:
> If we have died with him, we will also live with him.
> (2 Timothy 2:11)

Healing Mind, Soul and Spirit

How sick does one have to be in order to be anointed? The ritual states that the sacrament is for those of the faithful whose health is *seriously impaired* by sickness or old age. The sacrament is not given indiscriminately, yet the Church wishes to avoid restrictions that would deny anointing to those for whom it is intended. The sacrament is most fruitful when one is not too sick to participate in the prayers and ritual actions.

In the past we were sometimes too restrictive and often waited too long to celebrate the sacrament. The thrust of Vatican II's reform of this sacrament was to make it more available to the sick. Pope Paul VI, under whose direction the new rite was composed, was very clear and insistent on this point. In a homily at a communal Anointing of the Sick during Mass in St. Peter's Square on October 5, 1975, he said: "The revision's intent was to make the overall purposes of the rite clearer and to lead to a wider availability of the sacrament and to extend it—within reasonable limits—even beyond cases of mortal illness."

A person can be anointed before surgery when a serious illness or disability is the reason for the surgery. For example, the insertion of an artificial hip is occasion to ask for the sacrament. The anxiety before exploratory surgery to determine if cancer is present is a situation which Christ's power can heal in the sacrament. In these cases the person does not have to wait until he or she is in the hospital to request the sacrament. It is even preferable to celebrate the sacrament before going to the hospital. The person is better able to appreciate the prayers and symbols of the rite in a customary prayer situation with family or parish.

There are times when old age and the fears and isolation that can sometimes accompany it need to be brought to the healing and comforting presence of Christ in this sacrament. It is a powerful sign to a parish community to see senior members of the community place their limitations and dependence in the hands of Christ, who himself accepted our limitations and gave himself up to death that we may live. (At the same time, it is important to avoid the bias of identifying illness with certain age groups. Today, we do not automatically equate high numerical age with fragile health, weakness or inactivity. The Church should help fight such stereotypes.)

The sacrament is for all ages and all types of illness. Sick children who have sufficient use of reason to be strengthened by the sacrament can be anointed. Persons suffering from the disease of alcoholism or other addictions can be anointed, as can those who suffer from various mental disorders.

Does It Work?

"Will I experience healing?" This is the question everyone wants to ask. I have no hesitation whatsoever to answer yes. The sacrament is the prayer of the Church, the Body of Christ. Christ himself has assured us that whatever we ask the Father in his name will be granted.

Ask those who have received the sacrament if they have experienced healing. I know that I experienced healing when I was anointed. I know from speaking with many people who have been anointed by me or other priests that they are eager to tell of the healing that they experienced—and often the stories they tell are of wonderful, unexplainable physical healing. Other times the stories are less spectacular. But some form of healing does take place. It is not always physical healing, the healing of the medical profession. The sacrament is not a substitute for the work of doctors and nurses, drugs and hospitals. God's healing power works through the hands and intelligence of medical professionals, and we should pray that God guide these professionals also.

In the sacrament we pray that the sick be healed in body, in soul and in spirit. God knows more than we do what healing the sick person might need most: that a wound be healed; that fear turn to confidence; that loneliness disappear in the support of a praying Church; that bafflement in the face of all the *whys*—why me? why suffering? why now?—may turn into insight.

Ultimately, we hope that the Sacrament of Anointing will give us a better understanding of the mystery of a loving God who raises his crucified Son to display his victorious wounds as he sits forever at the Father's right hand.

FOR PRAYER

Healing God,
> you desire the health of all creation.
I give you thanks and I praise you
> for all the gifts and strengths you have given me.
Thank you especially for _____.
>> Give me your peace and wholeness. Heal me of _____.

Lord, make me an instrument of your peace.
Where there is hatred, let me sow love;
> where there is injury, pardon;
> where there is doubt, faith;
> where there is despair, hope;
> where there is darkness, light;
> and where there is sadness, joy.

Grant that I may not so much seek to be consoled

as to console;
to be understood, as to understand;
to be loved as to love.

For it is in giving that we receive;
it is in pardoning that we are pardoned;
and it is in dying that we are born to eternal life.
(Attributed to Saint Francis of Assisi)

FOR REFLECTION AND DISCUSSION

1) How are you an instrument of healing in today's world?

2) What areas of your life need healing?

3) In what circumstances would you ask to be anointed?

FOR FURTHER INFORMATION

Joseph Champlin, *Together by Your Side: A Book for Comforting the Sick and Dying*. Notre Dame, Ind.: Ave Maria Press, 1984.

Charles Gusmer, *And You Visited Me: Sacramental Ministry to the Sick and the Dying*. New York: Pueblo Publishing Company, 1984.

Joseph Moore, *Helping Skills for the Nonprofessional Counselor*. Cincinnati: St. Anthony Messenger Press, 1992.

Patti Normile, *Visiting the Sick: A Guide for Parish Ministers*. Cincinnati: St. Anthony Messenger Press, 1992.

Catechism of the Catholic Church, "The Anointing of the Sick" (#1499-1532).

CHAPTER EIGHT

A Ministry of Service:
Holy Orders

We arrive at the sacrament with which I am most familiar. I am
a priest; Holy Orders is something I live daily. Furthermore,
my principal ministry is to "make priests." I teach in a seminary
and help students prepare to celebrate the Eucharist, the
Sacrament of Reconciliation and the other sacraments.

The shape and function of ministry in the Catholic Church
is currently undergoing change and transition. The renewed
interest brought about by the Second Vatican Council in the
biblical roots of our faith and worship, together with the
rediscovery of the function of Baptism and the ministry of all
the faithful, have caused us to rethink the role that the ordained
minister plays in today's Church. While there are many
important things I could say that might help us find our way
during this time of transition, in these few pages I will try to
focus on what is most important to the way Catholics pray.

What Is a Priest?

I was tempted to begin this chapter by saying, "I am an
ordained priest and Jesus was not!" But that would be too much
of a shock. Non-Catholics and Catholics alike are so
accustomed to thinking of the Catholic Church as characterized
by priesthood, *as we know it today* (priests, bishops and the
pope), that it may be difficult to understand that this was not
the situation when the Church began. We usually think of Jesus
as a priest, the apostles as the first bishops and Saint Peter as
the first pope. It is important for our understanding of Holy
Orders to realize that priesthood, historically speaking (in
today's terms), developed slowly.

We often think of a priest as someone who stands between the people and God to offer sacrifice and worship for them. It is a surprise to many Catholics to learn that the Christian Scriptures do not speak of this type of priesthood. The Scriptures emphasize that only one mediator, Jesus Christ, is needed. Saint Thomas Aquinas said, "Only Christ is the true priest, the others being his ministers." In the New Testament we do not find the word *priest* applied to an ordained minister such as myself. We hear of the Levitical priesthood and the Jewish high priest (see, for example, Matthew 8:4, Mark 1:44). The pagan priesthood is also mentioned (for example, Acts 14:13).

The First Letter of Peter calls all the baptized priests: "Come to [Christ], a living stone, though rejected by mortals yet chosen and precious in God's sight, and like living stones, let yourselves be built into a spiritual house, to be a holy priesthood, to offer spiritual sacrifices acceptable to God through Jesus Christ.... But you are a chosen race, a royal priesthood, a holy nation, God's own people, in order that you may proclaim the mighty acts of him who called you out of darkness into his marvelous light" (1 Peter 2:4-5, 9).

It is not until the Letter to the Hebrews that we first see Jesus himself being referred to as a priest. It calls Jesus a "high priest" and compares his priesthood to the Levitical priesthood with which the Hebrews were familiar.

But there is no clear picture of individual priests in the early Christian community acting, as the Levitical priests did, as clerical mediators between God and the people, offering sacrifice on behalf of the community. Rather the entire Christian community was so identified with Jesus that they were his Body; they participated in *his* priesthood. By Baptism, Confirmation and Eucharist the Christians became the chosen race, royal priesthood, holy nation of 1 Peter.

Not everyone in the community, of course, had the same function or duties. Just as a human body has many parts with different functions, so the early community was organized with different officers so that it could grow and exercise its royal priesthood in an orderly fashion. We now see through the eyes of faith the origins of our current Church structures in the picture of Jesus and the apostles at the Last Supper. As the new *Catechism* says, "Through the ordained ministry, especially that of bishops and priests, the presence of Christ as head of the Church is made visible in the midst of the community of believers" (#1549). Various ministries or "orders" were found in the community.

What is a priest? I have been thinking seriously about this question for nearly fifty years. In 1948 I decided to become a priest. I was in the third grade at St. Anthony's School in Wichita, Kansas. At the age of nine I knew what a priest was and I wanted to be one! As soon as I completed the eighth grade, I went to the seminary and for the next thirteen years I worked at becoming a priest.

How times have changed! Boys and girls seldom make lifelong career choices in grade school anymore. Even most college students change their major on the average of three times and don't decide what they want to be till their junior year. There are so many more choices available today, it takes us more time to get our act together.

What is a priest? I could answer the question easily in 1948: The priest said Mass, heard confessions and taught people about God. (And once a week he appeared in the classroom at the Catholic grade school to check up on Sister and see if she was teaching us our catechism.)

Many things have changed since the 1940's. Today's seminaries are quite different from those of my day. But ask seminarians today why they want to be priests, and their answers won't be too different from the ones I gave in the third grade: They want to serve God's people in whatever way they can, especially by preaching the word of God, by bringing people together with forgiveness, healing and reconciliation, and by helping people experience Jesus in their lives.

Origins of Ordained Ministry

Through the centuries, this priestly ministry to the community has taken various forms. It is hard to reconstruct in full detail the growth and development of ministries or Orders in the community; in fact, it seems that the system was not uniform in all the lands to which the gospel spread. We do, however, find three Orders that are universal, and they are the key to our understanding of the Sacrament of Holy Orders today: (1) overseers, (2) elders, (3) special assistants.

In the early Church the overall management of the community was entrusted to an "overseer." He was responsible for the life and growth of the community. He accepted new members; he reconciled sinners; he led the community in its worship. In many ways he was something like the one we would call today "pastor of the parish."

A "council of elders" helped the overseer minister to the community. They aided him in his decisions and sometimes even stood in for him when he was absent. The elders helped the overseer with teaching, anointing the sick, missionary work, and establishing new communities in the neighboring towns and villages. By the fourth century, we see elders placed in charge of smaller, rural churches where they presided at Eucharist and received new members through the waters of Baptism.

In addition to the council of elders, the overseer had the help of special assistants, who served the overseer in meeting various practical needs of the community. They often took charge of the church finances, communications with the neighboring Churches and care for widows and orphans.

The overseer, the elders and the special assistants were members of the community. At the same time they were selected from the community and "ordained" for their special ministry. To ordain an overseer, the overseers of the neighboring Churches placed their hands on his head (the traditional gesture for giving the Holy Spirit) and prayed with the whole Church that the Spirit would guide him in governing this local Church.

The overseer, in turn, ordained the members of his council of elders by imposing hands on them and praying that the Spirit would strengthen them to carry out faithfully the work of the ministry he would entrust to them.

In this structuring of the community we find the origins of the Sacrament of Holy Orders. We speak of Orders in the plural, for these three different ministries still exist. The Greek word for "overseer" is *episkopos*, which becomes our words *episcopal* and *bishop*. An "elder" in Greek is *presbys*, which becomes *presbyter* and *priest* in English. The title given the special assistants was *diakonos* in Greek, *deacon* in English.

In addition to these three Orders—bishop, priest and deacon—there is the Order of the Faithful and the Order of the Catechumens. We belong to an "ordered" community. Not everyone has the same duties or ministry, but we are all called to be a holy people, a royal priesthood.

Shifting Job Descriptions

The "job description" of bishops, priests and deacons has changed through the centuries. During the Middle Ages, when many bishops became powerful political leaders, sometimes even leading armies into battle, they left the day-to-day ministry of their Church to the priests, and more and more of their responsibilities were assumed by the Bishop of Rome, the pope. The Order of Deacons, meanwhile, nearly disappeared from the Roman Church.

As a result of these job shifts, more and more responsibility fell upon the priest's shoulders. Often he was the only cleric visible to the ordinary people. The priest was looked upon as the one who received the power to say Mass and forgive sins for the Church at large. And these powers which he received at ordination were sometimes seen more as *personal* powers than as a ministry to be coordinated with that of the bishop of the local Church.

At the time of the Reformation there were those who felt that the emphasis on the sacrificial (Good Friday) dimension of the Eucharist diminished the "once and for all" value of the sacrificial death of Jesus. Consequently they began to speak of the Eucharist almost exclusively in terms of a holy meal (Holy Thursday). Catholics, on the other hand, continued to focus principally on the sacrificial aspects of the Eucharist, and consequently, leadership in the Catholic Church continued to be expressed in terms of priesthood. In the communities of the

Reformation the leader was more frequently called a pastor or minister.

When I began studying for the priesthood, I did not think of the Church as an "ordered community" or a "priestly people." I had never seen a deacon or a catechumen; I did not know what either was. I had seen a bishop only once (at my Confirmation). But I knew about priests! I saw lots of them: Priests said Mass; priests knew all about the Bible; priests knew the laws of the Church and could tell people what was right and wrong. The priests were the ones who served the people, and that's what I wanted to do.

But what is the role of the priest today?

The Priest and Today's Catholic Community

One way to understand the role of the priest today is to look at today's seminaries and see how priests are made. A seminary is a specialized graduate school; the students are college graduates. The academic training of the candidates begins with the study of Scripture, which roots the students in the Christian faith tradition. Courses in Church history show the different ways in which this revelation has been expressed in the Church as it spread to various cultures through the centuries. Systematic theology presents in an orderly (systematic) study of God, revelation, Jesus and the Church. The ordered functioning of the Church and the rights and duties of its members are examined in canon law. Liturgy and sacramental theology study how the mystery of Christ and the nature of the Church are revealed in worship. Moral theology examines this revelation to help us bring ourselves and the world to the fullness of life, justice and love.

A major difference between the seminary today and the seminary I attended back in the early 1960's is the degree of integration of academic and practical skills. In addition to the academic courses, listed above, there are now ministerial courses that help the seminarian acquire the skills he will need as a priest. He learns *how* to proclaim the gospel message (evangelization) and teach (catechetics) and preach (homiletics), how to counsel and comfort (pastoral counseling and psychology). These skills are learned not only in a classroom but also in the "real world"—actual ministering situations in parishes, schools and hospitals (field education, Clinical Pastoral Education, internship programs), where attitudes are formed, knowledge applied and skills practiced under the supervision of experienced ministers.

This academic and ministerial formation is integrated into a program of personal and spiritual growth by means of liturgical prayer, reflection on Scripture, spiritual direction and discussion with peers and teachers in integrating seminars. Today's seminarians need time to reflect on their life experiences and on their faith in order to integrate their studies, their life-style and their ministry. The whole process takes about five or six years after college. This long period of preparation culminates in the Rite of Ordination.

The Ordination of a Priest

Each of the three Holy Orders—deacons, priests, bishops—has its own specific Rite of Ordination. Here we will look only at the ordination of priests.

The ordination takes place in the context of the Eucharist. Again, the basic outline of the Eucharist—gathering, storytelling, meal sharing and commissioning—will be in evidence. The Rite of Ordination follows the storytelling, for each sacramental action is seen as our response to the word of God.

The ordaining bishop will first call forward those to be ordained. Ordination to the priesthood is not simply a private decision made by the individual being ordained; it is a call by the Church, a vocation (from the Latin *vocatio*, "summons"). After he is called forward, the candidate is officially chosen for the priesthood. And the bishop prays, "We rely on the help of the Lord God and our Savior Jesus Christ, and we choose this man, our brother, for priesthood in the presbyterial order" (*Ordination of a Priest*, #13).

The bishop will then give a homily explaining the

Scriptures that have just been read and will relate them to the role of the priest in the Church today. Following the homily, the candidate comes before the bishop and declares that he is ready to accept this ministry and promises obedience to the bishop and his successors.

Priestly ministry can only be fulfilled with the grace of the Holy Spirit; the next part of the ritual is a period of intense prayer and intercession. The candidate prostrates himself, lying flat on the ground in a gesture of humble submission while the bishop and the entire people of God call upon all the saints of heaven to intercede for us at this strategic moment.

Then comes the climax of the *Rite of Ordination*. The candidate kneels before the bishop and the bishop imposes his hands on the head of the candidate. This ancient and traditional gesture of invoking the Holy Spirit is the central act of the ordination rite. It is performed with great solemnity and in complete silence.

Following the imposition of hands the bishop sings the prayer of ordination. He recalls how God has always provided ministers for the Church and prays that God will "grant to this servant of yours the dignity of the priesthood. Renew within him the Spirit of holiness. As co-worker with the order of bishops, may he be faithful to the ministry that he receives from you, Lord God, and be to others a model of right conduct" (*Rite of Ordination*, #22).

In Roman times a person invested with a new office was given the symbols of that office. At this point in the ordination rite the new priest is invested with the stole and chasuble, the symbolic vestments of the presbyter. The bishop then anoints the newly ordained priest's hands, praying, "The Father anointed Our Lord Jesus Christ through the power of the Holy Spirit. May Jesus preserve you to sanctify the Christian people and to offer sacrifice to God" (*Rite of Ordination*, #24). The newly ordained then receives a paten and chalice, the vessels used for the celebration of the Eucharist.

The bishop embraces the new priest with a kiss of peace and all the other priests present come forward and welcome the new priest into their Order, the Order of the Presbyterate.

The Eucharist continues with the preparation of the gifts

and the Eucharistic Prayer. The newly ordained concelebrates
the Mass with the bishop.

Ministry and Baptism

When I was growing up Catholic in the 1940's, it seemed that
the priest was the only one who had any real ministry or
important role to play in the Church. The ministry received in
Baptism, "lay ministry," was unknown to me. The very word
minister was a "Protestant" word: Protestants had ministers;
Catholics had priests. I was brought up to think of the Church
in terms of priests and sisters—those who did the important
work of the Church—and the laity, the category that included
everybody else. Christian laity were those who were *not* priests
or sisters—those who ministered in the Church. And so I
understood *laity* to mean those *without* ministry.

For example, my mother helped a lot in the parish. Mom
was president of the Altar Society, which raised lots of money
for the parish, kept the church spotless and washed the altar
linens. She often took our car and drove the grade school sisters
to the doctor or shopping or wherever they needed to go (sisters
didn't drive in those days). But I never, at least in the days
before 1965, called this work "ministry."

The Second Vatican Council (1962-1965) was instrumental
in enlarging our understanding of "lay ministry." The bishops
turned to the Bible for language and categories to express their
thoughts.

On the earliest pages of the Christian Scriptures Paul speaks
of our Christian *diakonia*, which is translated in our English
Bibles as "ministry" or "service." In Romans, for example,
Paul speaks of our different ministries and says that we must
work together even as the members of a human body work
together for the good of the whole body. "For as in one body we
have many members, and not all the members have the same
function, so we, who are many, are one body in Christ, and
individually we are members one of another. We have gifts that
differ according to the grace given to us: prophecy, in
proportion to faith; ministry, in ministering; the teacher, in

teaching; the exhorter, in exhortation; the giver, in generosity; the leader, in diligence; the compassionate, in cheerfulness" (Romans 12:4-8). Paul tells us that all these gifts are for *diakonia*—service, ministry; with these gifts we are to serve the Lord.

Service and ministry are key themes of the Gospels. The Gospels do not speak of "lay ministers" or "clerical ministers." The language of the Gospels is more basic than these theological categories. The Gospels speak of "discipleship." Jesus says again and again, in many different ways: "Follow me. Be my disciples. Serve one another." Followers, disciples, servants and ministers: These are the Gospel categories.

Followers are those who walk with someone, those who follow someone as a disciple. I have heard many different explanations of what it means to be a Christian, but every explanation of Christianity has something to do with this basic notion of "following Jesus."

Disciples are those who learn, pupils. There is a cost, a tuition to be paid: "Whoever does not carry the cross and follow me cannot be my disciple" (Luke 14:27). Jesus said to his disciples, "If any want to become my followers, let them deny themselves and take up their cross and follow me" (Matthew 16:24).

Servants and ministers (*diakonoi*) are those who serve one another. As we follow Jesus and learn from him, what is the first lesson to be learned? "I came not to be served but to serve; not to be ministered unto but to minister" (see Matthew 20:26-28).

One reason Protestants were more at home with the word *minister* or *ministry* might stem from the fact that the King James translation of the Bible, which many Protestants used, more frequently translates the Greek *diakonia* as "ministry" than do the translations Catholics are likely to use, where the word is often translated as "service." For example, in the King James Version Matthew 20:26-28 says, "whosoever will be great among you, let him be your minister.... Even as the Son of man came not to be ministered unto, but to minister...." Catholics are more familiar with: "whoever wishes to be great among you shall be your servant, ...just as the Son of Man came not to be served but to serve...."

But whatever word we use, *service* or *ministry*, the sacramental sign of our discipleship is our Baptism. Jesus commanded, "Go therefore and make disciples of all nations, baptizing them in the name of the Father and of the Son and of the Holy Spirit..." (Matthew 28:19). Discipleship and Baptism go together.

When we follow Jesus and become disciples and accept Jesus in Baptism, we also accept his ministry. Christian discipleship and ministry are not something "added on" to Baptism or incidental to it; ministry is part and parcel of being Christian. Ministry is *not* just for a chosen few!

I believe that the biggest change brought about by the Second Vatican Council regarding the nature of the Catholic Church comes from the realization that the Order of the Faithful are really full and active members of the Church. They are no longer just there to "pray, pay and obey." "[B]y reason of their special vocation, the laity seek the Kingdom of God by engaging in temporal affairs and by ordering them according to the plan of God. They live in the world, in each and in all of the secular professions and occupations. They live in the ordinary circumstances of family and social life from which the very web of their existence is woven. They work for the sanctification of the world from within by fulfilling their own particular duties" (*Constitution on the Church*, #31).

We cannot understand the sacrament of Holy Orders if we think of the Church as the clergy and consider the mission of the Church the work of the priest alone. All of the baptized must accept and embrace their Christian ministry. I cannot predict or explain what ministry will do for you, but the testimony and experience of other ministers can assure you that ministry is more than just a task to be done. It will change the way you see others, the way you see yourself, the way you pray. It may even change your image of God.

109

For Prayer

Loving God, you have entrusted to us
  the continuing work of creation.
May I accept the ministry you have given me
  and bring your Good News to all I meet.
As I continue the ministry of Jesus
  may I never be an obstacle that keeps others
  from seeing you in all of creation.

For Reflection and Discussion

1) What are the qualities you look for in a priest or minister? How are these qualities different from those you would expect all baptized Christians to possess?

2) How do *you* build the Kingdom of God?

3) What is the relation between your Christian ministry and your employment?

For Further Information

Thomas O'Meara, *Theology of Ministry*. New York: Paulist Press, 1983.

Kenan Osborne, *Priesthood: A History of the Ordained Ministry in the Roman Catholic Church*. New York: Paulist Press, 1988.

David Power, *Gifts That Differ: Lay Ministries Established and Unestablished*. New York: Pueblo Publishing Company, 1980.

Edward Schillebeeckx, *Ministry: Leadership in the Community of Jesus Christ*. New York: Crossroad Publishing Company, 1981.

Catechism of the Catholic Church, "The Sacrament of Holy Orders" (#1536-1600).

CHAPTER NINE

A New Life Project: Marriage

What is marriage? It may seem that I am not the one to answer that question. I am not married; I have never been married and I don't intend to get married—which doesn't exactly qualify me to talk about marriage. Marriage is certainly a worthy topic for discussion. It is something that needs to be more clearly understood and more deeply appreciated. But this chapter is not about marriage, it is about the Sacrament of Marriage.

Although I am not married myself, I have experienced the Sacrament of Marriage. I have witnessed the marriages of friends and parishioners. I have participated in the wedding ceremony many times. In fact, the Sacrament of Marriage was the first sacrament that I experienced. Even before my infant Baptism I was born into a Christian marriage. What I am going to say about the sacrament is drawn from my experience of my parents and the many married couples with whom I have discussed the meaning of the sacrament—couples from the Christian Family Movement and Marriage Encounter—and the hundreds of couples whom I have helped prepare for marriage. These couples have often told me of the meaning which they find in this sacrament. As I have meditated on the passages of Scripture which couples have selected for their wedding ceremonies and asked me to preach about, I have come to the following conclusion: Marriage involves embarking on a new life project.

A New Life Project

We each have something that we want to do with our lives:

111

something we want to be, something we want to become. It may take us a while to find out what that "something" is, but eventually a life project forms, either consciously or unconsciously. And it seems to me that as people pursue this goal, whatever it may be—to be a skilled surgeon, to be the best kindergarten teacher that ever lived, to own a farm or whatever else they may see their life to be about—they sometimes encounter another human being to whom they are so attracted that the love of this other person supersedes all other life goals and ambitions. They undertake a new life project.

Little by little they decide that first on their agenda is now going to be the life, the happiness, the holiness of this other person. The good of this other takes precedence even over the desires and dreams they have for themselves. And when that other makes the same decision, together the two embark on a whole new adventure. It seems to me that this is the basic meaning of the Sacrament of Marriage.

The sacrament reveals the religious dimension of marriage. Besides the human, social and legal dimensions of marriage— the public sign that one gives oneself totally to this other person—sacramental marriage is also a public statement about God. As we have seen throughout this book, the celebration of each of the sacraments reveals something of this ultimate reality: who God is and who God is for us.

In the Scriptures the relationship between God and God's people is often described in terms of a marriage. The early Christians, reflecting on Christ's love for us, also used this image. Christ and the Church embrace in mutual love and self-giving, even as do husband and wife (see, for example, Ephesians 5:21-33). " 'For this reason a man will leave his father and mother and be joined to his wife, and the two will become one flesh.' This is a great mystery, and I am applying it to Christ and the church" (Ephesians 5:31-32).

Marriage in the Catholic Church

Marriage was around a long time before Jesus. His parents were married, and at least some of the apostles were married. For example, in all three of the Synoptic Gospels we hear of Peter's mother-in-law (Matthew 8:4; Mark 1:30; Luke 4:38). In the early Church, Christians got married like anyone else in the cultures where they lived. Gradually, Christians began to see that the loving union of husband and wife spoke to them not only about family values but also about God's values.

Historically speaking, it was not until the twelfth century that marriage took its place among the other ritual actions which we now name the seven sacraments. Throughout the Middle Ages there was no one wedding rite for Christians. The Catholic wedding ceremony that you might witness today dates in large part from about the sixteenth century.

The Catholic Wedding Ceremony

The rite has basically the same "shape" as all the other sacraments: gathering, storytelling, the sacramental action and commissioning. The gathering rites are similar to Sunday Mass, although the entrance procession is more elaborate. (Sometimes the entrance procession is so elaborate that it can steal the whole show, but I don't want to talk here about abuses.)

There was a time when the bride's father (owner) brought (dragged) the bride before the magistrate and there exchanged her for a sum of money (the bride price) paid by the groom. When the father no longer "sold" the girl, he "gave her away."

Many couples today find this symbol works against the meaning of their wedding ceremony. They want their ceremony to speak of families, couples, mutuality. The attendants enter together as couples; the groom enters with his father and mother and the bride with hers. At the front of the church they symbolically take leave of their parents and come together and speak a word of welcome to the assembly and invite them to pray that God will bless what they are about to do. The community is led in prayer by the presider and the gathering rites are brought to a close.

We are seated and listen to the readings from Scripture. Here again the rite will resemble the storytelling at Sunday

Mass. The couple selects Scripture passages according to the religious meaning they wish their wedding to express. Thus, the readings will sometimes refer to creation, for husband and wife are creating something new: a new life project, a new relationship, a new family. They are sign and sacrament of the new love project God embarked upon in creating the world. Or the readings will refer to the two becoming one: Husband and wife are joined in one flesh. Christian marriage is the sacrament which shows us God's desire to be one with us.

The couple then come before the Christian assembly and vow that their love will be a sign and sacrament of God's love for us. And the community prays for them and with them that we may receive this sign and that we may, by our faithful love, support their vows.

It is the bride and groom who perform the marriage. The priest, the attendants and the congregation *witness* what the bride and groom do. The bride and groom come forward and, before the congregation, the priest and the official witnesses, pronounce their vows. Today most couples choose to say the entire text of their vows to one another rather than merely saying "I do." They exchange rings as a sign of their love and fidelity and seal their vows with a kiss.

When two Catholics exchange these vows, they do so in the context of Eucharist. All that marriage says about God's love and desire to be one with us, Eucharist says in an even more all-embracing way. Bread and wine are brought to the altar, the priest proclaims the great prayer of praise and thanksgiving (the Eucharistic Prayer) and we approach the altar to receive Holy Communion—the living sign of God's desire to be one with us. And then a final blessing sends the bride and groom and the whole Christian community forth to bear witness to God's love for the world.

Annulments

Perhaps a paragraph about annulments is out of place in a "first look" at the sacraments. But the annulment process is so misunderstood by many non-Catholics and Catholics alike that

I feel a brief explanation is in order.

"An annulment is just a Catholic way of getting a divorce." I have heard this said by many people in many different circumstances (and there are times when I feel that there is an element of truth in this statement). Yet I remain convinced that an annulment is a very different thing from a divorce. Divorce is the legal dissolution of a marriage. An annulment is the legal declaration that a marriage never existed.

In order for a Christian marriage to take place the man and woman must be capable of entering into such a sacrament. The individuals must have the capacity to give such a gift. This capacity develops gradually. When we were children our parents taught us little by little to be generous—first with things, then with ourselves. We were taught to share toys, playthings, bicycles and birthday cake. Little by little, we learned to share our time and ourselves.

This gradual learning to give of ourselves is the necessary preparation for marriage. A person who has not journeyed sufficiently on the road to maturity and generosity is not capable of a true marriage, even though he or she may be quite capable of sharing an apartment or conceiving a child.

There are many reasons why two particular people cannot join their lives in the marriage project. It is not always a culpable lack of generosity. Sometimes it becomes apparent only years after the wedding ceremony that there was no marriage there in the first place. To declare publicly that the marriage never existed is what Catholics call an "annulment."

The Church does not want to say that a sacramental marriage comes to an end because we consider the love of the husband and wife to be a sign of God's unending love for us. God's love for us can never end in divorce. God is faithful even if we are not. The Church desires that even if one of the partners of a marriage is faithless to the marriage bond, the other, by remaining faithful, gives a powerful witness to the community of the way God loves us.

There are, however, times when looking back on a situation with more information now than we had then shows that what we thought was a marriage is not one. Such a decision or judgment is not made lightly. The decision can only be arrived at collectively, officially by the Church. It is a judicial process. The result of this judicial process (trial) is the declaration either that the marriage was valid or that the marriage was invalid (that is, that there never was a marriage). In other words, what we thought was a marriage is declared void and the contract is annulled.

An annulment does not make the children of the annulled marriage illegitimate. This is often difficult to understand unless one places oneself within the judicial and legal definitions of marriage, legitimacy and annulments.

Our Marriage Covenant With God

In each of the sacraments a window opens and we can glimpse the mystery of God and God's plan for the salvation of the world. In Christian marriage we see that God was not content to be alone, but embarked on a whole new life project. Out of love God created us and all that is. God is faithful no matter what. Whether we are faithful or faithless, God is faithful. Whether we wander away in sin or remain in the embrace of love, God is always there and is ever ready to embrace us.

This sacramental sign, which the husband and wife give to each other, they also give to the entire community of witnesses. I too have made commitments to God and God has made commitments to me. There are times when I wonder if God will be faithful. I have never seen God, but I can see the fidelity of Christian husbands and wives. Their love for each other is a sacramental sign and witness of God's love for me. I believe that our human lives are interconnected, like a fabric, woven together by many commitments. The fidelity of their commitment strengthens my own commitments.

This indeed is a great mystery. It is something that touches me deeply each time I experience a Christian wedding and each time I experience the sacramental love of husband and wife.

FOR PRAYER

Loving God,
you are the source of all life.
I thank you for the life you have given me.
I thank you for the parents who,
    in your provident love,
    gave me life and nurture.

Creator God,
    in your plan you decreed
    that it is not good for us to be alone.
Help me to love those whom you have entrusted to my care,
    especially _____.

Faithful God,
    help me to be faithful to my commitments
    especially to _____.

FOR REFLECTION AND DISCUSSION

1) What do you suppose leads couples to think about the sacramental dimension (the religious meaning) of their marriage as well as the human reality?

2) What makes a good marriage? Do you think your parents had (or have) a good marriage? If you are married yourself, do you think your marriage is a good marriage? What can you do to help strengthen marriage in our society? List four or five things a parish could do to help married couples grow in love and fidelity.

3) What do you understand as the difference between divorce and annulments?

FOR FURTHER INFORMATION

John Paul II, *On the Family (Familiaris consortio)*, December

15, 1981.

Joseph Champlin, *Together for Life*. Notre Dame, Ind.: Ave Maria Press, 1988.

Theodore Mackin, *What is Marriage?* New York: Paulist Press, 1982.

Thomas Richstatter, O.F.M., *Before You Say 'I Do': Four Things to Remember When Planning Your Wedding Liturgy*. Cincinnati: St. Anthony Messenger Press, 1989.

Catechism of the Catholic Church, "The Sacrament of Matrimony" (#1601-1666).

CHAPTER TEN

Catholic Funerals:
Baptism Revisited

The funeral rite is not one of the Church's seven sacraments. A chapter on funerals may therefore be out of place in this book. But there is a deeper reason why I would like to say a word here about funerals: With funerals we return to the beginning. At the funeral of a Catholic we confidently celebrate Christ's paschal mystery. We return again to the promise of Baptism:

> In the face of death, the Church confidently proclaims that God has created each person for eternal life and that Jesus, the Son of God, by his death and resurrection, has broken the chains of sin and death that bound humanity. (*Order of Christian Funerals*, #1)

We are back at our starting point: the humanity of Jesus, the original sacrament. As the Christian journey begins with Jesus, so it ends with Jesus in the proclamation of the paschal victory.

Perhaps it is more accurate to say that the journey begins rather than ends, for truly Christian life begins with our passage from this life to the next. Catholics have always celebrated the feasts and memorials of saints not on the day when they were born into this life, but on the day when they were born into eternal life, that is, the day of their martyrdom or death.

What Does the Funeral Look Like?

The Catholic *Order of Christian Funerals* embraces several groups of rites to accompany the bereaved and the faith community in their grief and loss. These rites help us to remember the promise of Saint Paul:

> Do you not know that all of us who have been baptized
> into Christ Jesus were baptized into his death?
> Therefore we have been buried with him by baptism
> into death, so that, just as Christ was raised from the
> dead by the glory of the Father, so we too might live in
> newness of life.
> For if we have been united with him in a death like
> his, we shall also be united with him in a resurrection
> like his. (Romans 6:3-5)

As death approaches, ritual prayers support the dying. The
Church prepares Catholics for the journey from this life to the
next with viaticum (from the Latin word for "traveling
provisions"). "The celebration of the Eucharist as viaticum,
food for the passage through death to eternal life, is the
sacrament proper to the dying Christian" (*Pastoral Care of the
Sick*, #175).

The Church provides ritual prayers for the moment of
death—prayers for both the deceased and the bereaved. After
the body has been prepared for burial, we pray with the family
and friends as they gather in the presence of the body. The faith
community gathers and keeps watchful vigil until the time for
the funeral. The prayers for these vigils are modeled on a
traditional and ancient form of prayer in the Church, the
Liturgy of the Hours.

The Liturgy of the Hours

When I was a child, Mass was celebrated daily but few people
in our parish attended. Rather, large crowds gathered several
evenings a week for "devotions": Saint Anthony devotions on
Tuesdays, the Way of the Cross on Fridays and Our Lady of
Fatima devotions on Saturdays.

With the relaxation of the Communion fast and the
possibility of evening Masses (together with changes in the
Mass itself which caused the Eucharist to be more

"devotional"), the principal time when Catholics gather for prayer on weekdays is for Mass. But the decreasing number of priests is causing many parishes to reevaluate daily Mass and to return to the ancient practice of the Liturgy of the Hours.

Many Catholics have never heard of the Liturgy of the Hours or the Divine Office (or the Breviary, as it was formerly called), and many who have heard of it associate this prayer with priests or monks and nuns. The Second Vatican Council reminded us that the Liturgy of the Hours is not the exclusive preserve of one group in the Church, but belongs to all the faithful.

It is, as the name implies, a way in which the praises of God are sung throughout the hours of the day. The principal and most traditional times for praying are morning and evening: Morning Praise (Lauds) and Evensong (Vespers). These "hours" consist of (1) gathering rites, (2) psalms and hymns of praise, (3) reading from the word of God and (4) intercessory prayer.

At a typical Evening Prayer in a parish, Catholics gather around the paschal candle and pray that, as the light of the day grows dim, the light of Christ will continue to illumine their hearts. They then sit and sing or recite several (often three) psalms and biblical canticles praising God and thanking God for the blessings of the day. Then a reader proclaims a passage of Scripture, usually from the daily lectionary. A homily and a period of silent reflection follow. In response to the word of God, we join with Mary, the Mother of God, and sing her Magnificat (Luke 1:46-55): "My soul magnifies the Lord,/and my spirit rejoices in God my Savior." Evening Prayer concludes with prayers of petition and thanksgiving for the gifts of the day. We gather all our prayers into the Lord's Prayer.

The vigil for the deceased follows this basic outline: gathering, songs or psalms, Scripture and intercessions. The vigil is often a time to give expression to our grief and to eulogize the deceased.

The Funeral Mass

The ritual provides for prayers for the transferral of the body to the church and for the funeral Mass. As the body of the deceased enters the church and passes the baptismal pool, water is taken from the pool and sprinkled on the casket. In this simple gesture we have summed up the meaning of the Catholic funeral rites: For those who have died with Christ in the waters of Baptism, the "second death" can hold no terror: "If we have died with him we will also live with him" (2 Timothy 2:11b).

The casket is then covered with a white cloth, reminding us of the garment we received at Baptism. "You have become a new creation, and have clothed yourself in Christ. See in this white garment the outward sign of your Christian dignity. With your family and friends to help you by word and example, bring that dignity unstained into the everlasting life of heaven" (*Rite of Baptism for Children*, #99).

The body is brought into the church and we hear the word of God, the word which assures us of Christ's victory over sin and death. We celebrate the Eucharistic meal which proclaims and brings about our union with the risen Christ: "I am the living bread that came down from heaven. Whoever eats of this bread will live forever..." (John 6:51).

The body is honored with incense. In the Roman culture (which shaped the formation of our Catholic burial rites), burning incense was often carried ahead of a person passing through the streets of Rome so that the sweet fragrance would mask the odors of the city. As this luxury could only be afforded by the rich, the custom came to be associated with honoring those of noble birth. In the funeral rites the fragrant incense gives honor to the body of the deceased, which became a dwelling of the Holy Spirit through the sacraments of initiation. As we see the smoke of the incense rise toward heaven, we ask that our prayers for the deceased may ascend before the throne of the living God.

The community, filled with hope in the resurrection, accompanies the body of the deceased to the place of burial for the "Rite of Committal." The Lord Jesus Christ, by his own three days in the tomb, has "made the grave a sign of hope that promises resurrection even as it claims our mortal bodies" (*Order of Christian Funerals*, #218). Here at the grave the community makes its final gestures of leave-taking. The Christian journey is completed.

FOR PRAYER

> Loving Jesus, for our sake
>   you opened your arms on the cross
>   to put an end to death
>   and reveal the resurrection.
> In your death my own fear of death has been conquered.
> Each day help me to die to sin,
>   to die to all that keeps me from following you,
>   to die especially to _____.
>
> May I observe all that I promised in Baptism
>   so that I may be filled in heaven
>   with the blessings of the most high Father
>   and on earth with the blessing of the beloved Son
>   with the most Holy Spirit, the Paraclete.
> May I strive after those things which you have promised.
> (Saint Francis of Assisi)[1]
>
> Saint Joseph, patron of a peaceful death, pray for me.

FOR REFLECTION AND DISCUSSION

1) Has anyone close to you died? Do you remember the funeral? Which elements of the funeral were a positive experience for you? Which elements of the funeral were a negative experience?

2) How does a Roman Catholic funeral compare with funerals in other Churches?

3) In the past, Catholic funerals were perceived by some to be excessively morbid, focused on the fear of damnation.

Catholic funerals today emphasize Christian hope in the Resurrection. Now they are sometimes criticized for being "too happy." Do you find this to be the case? Why or why not?

FOR FURTHER INFORMATION

Richard Rutherford, *The Death of a Christian: The Order of Christian Funerals*. Collegeville, Minn.: The Liturgical Press, Pueblo Books, 1991.

Catechism of the Catholic Church, "Christian Funerals" (#1680-1990.

Notes

[1] Adapted from "The Testament" in *Francis and Clare: The Complete Works*, translated by Regis J. Armstrong, O.F.M. Cap., and Ignatius C. Brady, O.F.M. (New York: Paulist Press, 1982).

CHAPTER ELEVEN

Four Treasures in the Attic:
The Second Vatican Council

Catholics often want to know why things are not the way they used to be. I am often asked to address this question by parish and diocesan groups across the country. I have developed a talk which I call "Four Treasures in the Attic" which many older Catholics have found helpful (or so they told me).

Even though this book is for those who want to know how Catholics pray *now*, I will try to explain briefly what I find to be the four major reasons why Roman Catholics celebrate the sacraments differently now than they did thirty years ago.

Changing the Friar's Chapel

In the years following the Second Vatican Council, many chapels and churches were renovated in order to accommodate the new liturgy. This was often accompanied by a certain amount of stress in a parish (not unlike the stress that can take place in a family whose home is being remodeled).

In 1972 the chapel of the Franciscan seminary where I was teaching needed to be renovated. It had numerous side altars (each with its own tabernacle) for the daily "private" Masses of priest faculty members. The space around the main altar was too small to permit concelebration. The aisles needed to be widened to accommodate the processions for the reception of Communion from the cup, and so on.

A competent architect was hired and preliminary plans made. One of the architect's proposals was to paint the walls a solid color. This meant painting over several pictures of Franciscan saints who had graced the walls for as long as the chapel had stood there.

As you can imagine, some in the community thought that painting over these pictures was a desecration. Art was being destroyed. The community, holy and fraternal as we were, had several "discussions" (heated arguments) as to whether or not the pictures in question had any artistic merit. To help us end this argument, our friar guardian decided to invite the curator of the local art museum to come to the seminary and see whether these pictures had any artistic value.

The appointed day arrived, as did the expert from the art museum. He was taken to the chapel and, in approximately forty-five seconds, he determined that the art world would be better served if the pictures in question disappeared! Since we had paid good money for his coming (too good for forty-five seconds of work!), we asked the curator if he would be willing to see if we had *any* real art in the building. He agreed to do so.

He toured the corridors, the study halls, the dining rooms and the dormitories. He went through the entire building, top to bottom, and found that we did have four paintings of artistic merit, four paintings that were indeed good art. I am embarrassed to say that he found all four of these treasures in the seminary attic! We took the treasures from the attic and placed them at strategic and appropriate places throughout the building, where they could be enjoyed and appreciated.

This story provides the context for what I want to say in this chapter about the changes in the liturgy.

What Is Behind the Changes?

One day during the Second Vatican Council, good Pope John XXIII gathered with all the cardinals and bishops, and they exchanged their silk cassocks for bibbed overalls. (No one else recalls this, but I remember it clearly!) They went up to the attic of the Vatican to see if they had stored away any treasures that should be taken down and returned to the faithful. As times change, sometimes good stuff gets put away and forgotten. And indeed, they too found four treasures.

The four treasures they found were: Baptism, the Bible, Holy Thursday and the world.

126

Baptism

The Second Vatican Council certainly did not invent Baptism. Baptism has been around as long as the Church. But in a real sense the Second Vatican Council took Baptism out of the attic. The rites of Christian initiation I described in Chapter Two were unknown to Catholics thirty years ago.

When I was a child I viewed the Church as divided into two classes of people: the laity and the clergy, the unordained and the ordained. Baptism, of course, took away original sin; but really to be an active member of the Church one needed to be ordained. The Church, in my mind, was identified with the clergy: "Father says" equaled "the Church teaches." (There are times when I wish this part of the scenario would return, but it is gone forever!) Only the ordained knew what was going on; only the ordained seemed to have a role to play and a ministry to fulfill.

I thought that the command of Jesus at the end of the Gospel of Matthew was "go and baptize all nations. Then look at those whom you have baptized, pick out a few really good ones and make them disciples." This, of course, is not at all what the Gospel says. The Gospel equates Baptism and discipleship. Each of the baptized is to be a disciple. All the baptized have a ministry in the Church. This is the vision that has been restored by the Second Vatican Council. Baptism came out of the attic.

When you take something out of the attic, for example, a picture that you want to hang on the wall, you may have to rearrange the rest of the pictures. Our faith is like that also. Sometimes when we add a new element, we must rearrange the elements that were already there.

To some it seemed that the new prominence given to the sacrament of Baptism caused the sacrament of Holy Orders to be neglected. Some even thought that the Second Vatican Council caused the decline in vocations to the priesthood. This, of course, is not the case. Rediscovering the importance of my Baptism has not caused me to stop wanting to be a priest.

127

The Bible

The Second Vatican Council did not write the Bible. The Bible, like Baptism, is as old as the Church (and much of it is much older). Before the Council, however, the Bible did not play a very prominent role in the life of Catholics.

I still remember the day (I was in the fourth grade) when the Bible salesman came to our door, and my Mom and Dad purchased our family Bible. It was a beautiful book, the most beautiful book we owned. It was given a prominent place in the living room. Mother carefully recorded all our important family events—births and deaths, ordinations and weddings—in the "Family Record" section. It was a treasured book, but it was a book which we never read!

In school I learned about Jesus from a Bible history, which synthesized the Gospels to bring them into harmony with one another. The teachings of Jesus I learned not from the Bible but from the catechism. The *Baltimore Catechism* was my most used Catholic book, the one I learned to quote by heart, chapter and verse.

During these years, those of us who went to daily Mass remember that during the week the priest usually wore black vestments and "said" the daily Mass for the dead. This Mass had two fixed Scripture readings: the Epistle and the Gospel. Consequently, we heard these same two readings nearly every day.

Not long ago, when I was giving a talk to a large group of religious sisters at their motherhouse (women my age and older), I did some mathematical calculations ahead of time and figured out approximately how many times they would have heard those two Scripture passages at daily Mass. It was a lot! I asked the assembled sisters how many knew what those two readings were. No one remembered!

I tell this story not to make fun of these sisters; quite the contrary. They were among the most educated and most devout Catholics. I tell this story to remind us (who have now become accustomed to the daily lectionary) that in the days before the

Council, Scripture simply was not as important for us as it is today. If the content of the Gospel reading at Mass was not important in the lives of these sisters, I think the point is clearly made that the Bible did not play a significant role for most Catholics in their celebration of the sacraments.

The Second Vatican Council took the Bible out of the attic and put it back into the hands of every Catholic.

Holy Thursday

As we saw in Chapter Four, in the days before the Second Vatican Council we understood the Mass primarily in terms of sacrifice (Good Friday). It was largely due to the reforms of the Council that Catholics have returned to frequent Communion and to the experience of the Eucharist as a sacred meal. The Second Vatican Council got "Holy Thursday" out of the attic and placed it alongside Good Friday.

The results of this change are still being experienced in parishes across the country. And, as the Easter Sunday image is added to the Holy Thursday and Good Friday images, we can expect even greater changes in our understanding of the Eucharist and further changes in our eucharistic devotion.

We saw many of the implications of getting Holy Thursday out of the attic in Chapter Four, so I will not repeat them here.

The World

Perhaps the greatest treasure which the Vatican Council found in the attic (and the treasure which has caused the greatest change in the way we Catholics pray) was the world. In the time before the Council, I was taught to *despise* the things of this world. The world was a "valley of tears," sort of a spiritual boot camp whose sufferings and trials strengthened me and prepared me one day to join the ranks of the heavenly host. Religion was to keep me unstained by this world and to get me safely to heaven. Three things were to be avoided at all cost: the world, the flesh and the devil.

The Vatican Council took the world out of the attic and proclaimed its beauty and positive value. Creation is to be treasured and cared for. All created things are interrelated. Ecology, acid rain, the environment, the extinction of species: These are not concerns of a few marginal people. These are religious issues which are at the very heart of our Catholic faith.

With the world out of the attic, we rediscovered the meaning of the Incarnation. Christ took flesh and became truly human: God became mixed up with all that God created. Liturgy and Catholic prayer began to rediscover its bodily character. We began to eat real bread and to drink real wine—all of us. The waters of Baptism became more than just a few drops of water on the forehead.

For Catholics the Incarnation means that the very stuff of this earth has been taken up into the reign of God. The things of this earth are not distractions from praying or hindrances to our worship, but can become the very instrument—way, medium, means, symbols, sacraments—for liturgical prayer.

Catholics worship not just with their heads but with the things of the earth: bread and wine, water and oil, coming together and going apart, standing still and processing, lighting candles and smelling flowers, even dust and ashes! That's *liturgical* prayer—prayer with the body, the earth, ritual, song, celebration.

In recent years we have come to see our daily work as more than a way to make a living. Our "work" is a participation in God's work at the dawn of time.

On the very first pages of the Bible we see God *working*: working in the garden, watering dust into clay and forming the earthling from the earth. And we are told that we are created in "the image of God"—in the image of the God who works, makes, forms, reconciles, calls to full life. We are created in the image of this "working God." Our task, our principal Christian ministry, is to work and transform the earth. Our work continues the creative activity of God.

Farmers can see their work as continuing the work of God in the garden of the Genesis story. Doctors and those involved in health care participate by their work in the life-sustaining activity of God. Artists and builders continue God's creation. Social workers and politicians continue God's work of justice and reconciliation. But whatever our work—teaching school or cooking hamburgers, building a fence or waterproofing a basement—our work should be more than merely the means to get enough money to buy things. Our daily work must be taken up into the Lord's Prayer, "Thy kingdom come!"

FOR PRAYER

Loving God, womb and source of all life,
    you have created all that exists.
Help me to appreciate
    and to treasure the wonders of your creation.
May I see your beauty in all created things.
May I care for creation and preserve it
    as co-creator with you.
You have created us in your image
    to till the earth and preserve it.
Help me in my work
    that I may bring your creation to completion.
Help me especially to _____.

Christ yesterday and today,
the beginning and the end,
Alpha and Omega,
all time belongs to you
and all the ages.
To you be glory and power
through every age for ever. Amen.
(Adapted from the Easter Vigil)

Ageless Christ,
    keep me young in every age
    that I may grow with your Church.
Help me to let loose of the past
    and to reach out to _____.

FOR REFLECTION AND DISCUSSION

1) Do you think that Baptism actually makes a difference in a person's life?

2) Is the Bible your most important book? Why or why not?

3) In what ways do you make a conscious effort to conserve creation? Do you reuse, reduce and recycle?

FOR FURTHER INFORMATION

Bernard Botte, *From Silence to Participation: An Insider's View of Liturgical Renewal.* Washington, D.C.: The Pastoral Press, 1988.

Annibale Bugnini, *The Reform of the Liturgy (1948-1975).* Collegeville, Minn.: The Liturgical Press, 1990.

Peter Hebblethwaite, *Paul VI: The First Modern Pope.* New York: Paulist Press, 1993.

Catechism of the Catholic Church, "The Sacrament of Baptism" (#1213-1284); "Sacred Scripture" (#101-141); "The Paschal Banquet" (#1382-1405); "The Mystery of Creation" (#295-421).

Conclusion:
The End of the Journey

Thank you for coming with me on this tour through the sacraments. I hope that our journey together has been helpful.

When we participate in a sacramental celebration, we are not merely passive witnesses. We are there open to be touched by the presence of God. I hope this book has helped you in some small way to know what we are doing when we gather to celebrate the sacraments, so that you too may be graced by God's presence.

I want to thank the many non-Catholics who have asked me questions about the way Catholics pray. I have tried to answer those questions in this book. I would also like to thank the many Catholics who have asked me questions, especially those who have told me of their reservations about the changes and their anger with the liturgy as revised by the Second Vatican Council. Their conversation and concerns have also shaped this book.

As I look back on our journey together I am impressed by two central characteristics of Catholic prayer which have resurfaced time and time again in these chapters: (1) Catholics pray with their whole body; (2) Catholic prayer, for all its seeming complexity, is actually very simple.

Many people are attracted to the Catholic Church by the beauty and majesty of its liturgical ceremonies. And we Catholics do have magnificent rites. The pope's midnight Mass each Christmas is viewed by a bigger TV audience than any TV evangelist could ever hope for!

But, while I enjoy magnificent architecture and musical masterpieces, I find the real beauty of the liturgy not in the golden cups and jewelled vestments, but in the very ordinary

133

everydayness of it all—eating and drinking, standing and sitting, shaking hands and keeping quiet.

I'm with Saint Augustine. When his fourth-century congregation asked: "What happened to the miracles? Feeding thousands with five loaves and raising the dead to life?" Augustine asked them to consider the grain of wheat, falling into the ground and producing stalk and blade. Where can you find a greater miracle than that?

The liturgy is the principal element in my life that has helped me develop a sense of reverence and a spirit of wonder and awe at the presence of God in the ordinary events of daily life. The liturgy is filled with this ordinaryness. For example, on Holy Thursday, the day when we solemnly recall the Lord's Supper and the incomprehensible miracle of God's continuing presence among us, what do we do at the solemn liturgy to recall so great a mystery? In the midst of gold vestments and vessels, we wash feet. We wash feet! It doesn't get more ordinary than dirty feet!

That's why I'm a Catholic: My Catholic faith gives me eyes to see that the ordinary is divine. And I can pray with Saint Francis of Assisi:

Praised be you, my Lord, with all your creatures,
especially Sir Brother Sun,
Who is the day and through whom you give us light.
He is beautiful and radiant with great splendor;
    and bears the likeness of you, Most High One.
Praised be you, my Lord, through Sister Moon and the
stars,
    in heaven you formed them clear and precious and
      beautiful.
Praised be you, my Lord, through Brother Wind,
    and through the air, cloudy and serene,
    and every kind of weather
through which you give sustenance to your creatures.
Praised be you, my Lord, through Sister Water,
    which is very useful and humble and precious and
      chaste.
Praised be you, my Lord, through Brother Fire,

through whom you light the night,
and he is beautiful and playful and robust and strong.
Praised be you, my Lord, through our Sister Mother
Earth,
    who sustains and governs us,
and who produces varied fruits with colored flowers
and herbs.[7]

Notes

[1] Adapted from *Francis and Clare: The Complete Works*, translated by Regis J. Armstrong, O.F.M., and Ignatius C. Brady, O.F.M. (New York: Paulist Press, 1982).